The World's Best Tax Havens 2014/2015

How to Cut Your Taxes to Zero & Safeguard Your Financial Freedom

L Hadnum

IMPORTANT LEGAL NOTICES:

WealthProtectionReportTM
TAX GUIDE - "The World's Best Tax Havens 2014/2015"

Published by:
WealthProtectionReport.co.uk
Email: sales@wealthprotectionreport.co.uk

11th Edition: March 2014

Copyright
Copyright © WealthProtectionReport.co.uk All rights reserved.

No part of this publication may be reproduced or transmitted in any form or by any means (electronically or mechanically, including photocopying, recording or storing it in any medium by electronic means) without the prior permission in writing of the copyright owner except in accordance with the provisions of the Copyright, Designs and Patents Act 1988 or under the terms of a licence issued by the Copyright Licensing Agency Ltd, 90 Tottenham Court Road, London, W1P 0LP. All applications for the written permission of the copyright owner to reproduce or transmit any part of this Tax Guide should be sent to the publisher.
Warning: Any unauthorised reproduction or transmission of any part of this Tax Guide may result in criminal prosecution and a civil claim for damages.

Trademarks
The logo "WealthProtectionReportTM" is a trademark of WealthProtectionReport.co.uk. All other logos, trademarks, names and logos in this Tax Guide may be trademarks of their respective owners.

DISCLAIMER

1. Please note that this tax guide is intended as general guidance only for individual readers and does NOT constitute accountancy, tax, legal, investment or other professional advice. WealthProtectionReport and the author accept no responsibility or liability for loss which may arise from reliance on information contained in this tax guide.

2. Please note that tax legislation, the law and practices by government and regulatory authorities (for example, HM Revenue and Customs) are constantly changing and the information contained in this tax guide is only correct as at the date of publication. We therefore recommend that for accountancy, tax, investment or other professional advice, you consult a suitably qualified accountant, tax specialist, independent financial adviser, or other professional adviser. Please also note that your personal circumstances may vary from the general examples given in this tax guide and your professional adviser will be able to give specific advice based on your personal circumstances.

3. This tax guide covers UK taxation mainly and any references to 'tax' or 'taxation' in this tax guide, unless the contrary is expressly stated, are to UK taxation only. Please note that references to the 'UK' do not include the Channel Islands or the Isle of Man. Addressing all foreign tax implications is beyond the scope of this tax guide.

4. Whilst in an effort to be helpful, this tax guide may refer to general guidance on matters other than UK taxation, WealthProtectionReport and the author are not experts in these matters and do not accept any responsibility or liability for loss which may arise from reliance on such information contained in this tax guide.

CONTENTS

Introduction

1 How Tax Havens Can Help You

2 The World's Best Tax Havens

Andorra

Anguilla

The Bahamas

Barbados

Belize

Bermuda

The British Virgin Islands (BVI)

Campione

The Cayman Islands

The Channel Islands

The Cook Islands

Costa Rica

Cyprus

Dubai

Eastern Europe

Gibraltar

Hong Kong

Ireland

Isle of Man

Liechtenstein

Malta

Monaco

Panama

Seychelles

Singapore

St Kitts and Nevis

Switzerland

Turks and Caicos Islands (TCI)

3	Living in a Tax Haven
4	How Offshore Trusts Can Help You
5	Escaping the Taxman's Clutches
6	How an Offshore Company Can Help You
7	How Big Companies and the Rich Use Tax Havens
8	Protecting Your Privacy with Nominees
9	How to Avoid the EU Savings Tax Directive
10	The Tremendous Benefits of Double Tax Treaties
11	Other Important Tax Haven Benefits

ABOUT THE AUTHOR

Lee Hadnum LLB ACA CTA is an international tax specialist. He is a Chartered Accountant and Chartered Tax Adviser and is the Editor of the popular tax planning website:

www.wealthprotectionreport.co.uk

Lee is also the author of a number of best selling tax planning books including:

- **Tax Planning Techniques Of The Rich & Famous** - Essential reading for anyone who wants to use the same tax planning techniques as the most successful Entrepreneurs, large corporations and celebrities

- **The Worlds Best Tax Havens 2014/2015** – 220 page book looking at the worlds best offshore jurisdictions in detail

- **Non Resident & Offshore Tax Planning 2014/2015** – Offshore tax planning for UK residents or anyone looking to purchase UK property or trade in the UK. A comprehensive guide.

- **Tax Planning With Offshore Companies & Trusts: The A-Z Guide** - Detailed analysis of when and how you can use offshore companies and trusts to reduce your UK taxes

- **Tax Planning For Company Owners 2014/2015** – How company owners can reduce income tax, corporation tax and NICs

- **How To Avoid CGT In 2014/2015** – Tax planning for anyone looking to reduce UK capital gains tax

- **Buy To Let Tax Planning 2014/2015** – How property investors can reduce income tax, CGT and inheritance tax

- **Asset Protection Handbook** – Looks at strategies to ringfence your assets in today's increasing litigious climate

- **Working Overseas Guide** – Comprehensive analysis of how you can save tax when working overseas

- **Double Tax Treaty Planning** – How you can use double tax treaties to reduce UK taxes

INTRODUCTION

Offshore tax planning has become increasingly popular over the years as more and more wealthy individuals seek to escape the high taxes imposed in many of the wealthy developed countries.

Offshore tax planning has two key components:

- Understanding the tax rules in your current country of residence, and
- Understanding the tax regimes of other countries.

This book is concerned mainly with the second component: identifying countries that have low tax rates and offer you the opportunity to pay less tax.

We'll be looking at where you should go and live or buy property if you want to pay as little tax as possible. We'll also look at how offshore trusts, companies and other structures can be used.

Wealth Warning!

Always remember that your home country's tax laws will affect your ability to use tax havens.

Always seek professional advice before you act. International tax is a complex area and no book can cover all the angles.

What is a Tax Haven?

At the outset we need to explain what is meant by the phrase 'tax haven' and summarise the benefits they offer before identifying the countries and tax planning techniques in more detail.

A tax haven is simply a country that allows you to reduce the amount of tax you pay.

This is a tax haven at its most basic and, although pretty obvious, it's worth bearing in mind what their purpose is without getting bogged down in the details.

Let's state at the beginning that there is nothing wrong with using tax havens provided you are careful not to break any rules in your country of residence.

Many people use tax havens to hide their money from the tax authorities in their home countries. This is not only illegal, it's foolish because one day you probably will get caught and could end up with substantial fines or even a jail sentence.

However, if you have the legal right to use a tax haven you would be foolish not to take advantage of all the opportunities you can to maximise your wealth.

There are three main types of tax haven:

- Nil-tax havens
- Foreign source exempt havens
- Low-tax havens

Nil-Tax Havens

These are simply countries that do not have any of the three main direct taxes:

- No income tax or corporation tax
- No capital gains tax, and
- No inheritance tax

Many of the nil tax havens you've probably heard of or read about in novels. You may even have holidayed in some of them. They include:

- The Cayman Islands
- St Kitts and Nevis
- Dubai
- Monaco
- The Bahamas
- Bermuda
- Vanuatu
- The Turks & Caicos Islands
- Anguilla

Although there are no taxes in these jurisdictions, the tax haven governments still need to generate some revenue to provide public services. They may therefore impose small fees for company incorporation documents or annual registration fees for companies.

However, these charges are fixed and usually small. If you're looking at living in one of these jurisdictions, most of these charges won't apply and you may able to live with little state involvement in your affairs. The only tax charges that would then affect you would be import duties or local sales taxes.

Foreign Source Exempt Havens

These countries do levy taxes and sometimes they can be pretty high. However, what makes them tax havens is the fact they only tax you on *locally derived income*.

In other words, if all your income is derived outside the tax haven you will not pay any tax. Good examples of foreign source exempt tax havens are:

Panama
Costa Rica
Hong Kong
Seychelles
Singapore

This type of tax haven exempts from tax any income earned from foreign sources, provided (and this is crucial) the foreign income source does not involve any local business activity.

For example, you couldn't set up a consultancy business that was run from Panama and claim that the income generated shouldn't be subject to tax there.

Some of the other tax havens don't even allow a company to conduct business internally if any tax advantages are to be claimed.

Jurisdictions such as Panama and Gibraltar would require a company to decide at the time of incorporation whether it was allowed to do local business (and therefore taxed on its worldwide profits), or only foreign business and therefore free from taxation.

Low-Tax Havens

The final group of tax havens are countries that do have a system of taxation and impose taxes on residents' worldwide income. You may be wondering why these are still classed as tax havens. There are two main reasons:

- Some countries may have special concessions that offer considerable tax advantages in *special situations* (such as for capital gains tax avoidance).
- Clever use of double tax treaties that countries enter into with each other may allow you to *lower* your tax bill.

The problem with the well-known nil-tax havens is most developed countries do not have treaties with them. When planning your tax affairs it may be more tax efficient to use a low-tax haven, combined with a double tax treaty, than simply rely on a nil-tax haven.

Example

Let's say you own shares in a company listed on the New York Stock Exchange. For commercial reasons (in other words, non-tax reasons) you want to set up a holding company to own the shares. You could use one of the traditional tax havens such as the Bahamas or the Cayman Islands. The problem with using these countries is that US withholding tax will be deducted from dividends at rates of up to 30%.

However, if you use one of the recognised holding company jurisdictions, such as Belgium or Denmark, there may be very little tax deducted in the US. Good examples of low-tax havens are:

- Cyprus
- The United Kingdom
- Barbados
- Switzerland
- Denmark
- Belgium
- The Netherlands
- Austria

Other Important Factors to Consider

When looking at tax havens, although the amount of tax they levy is obviously crucial, this is not the only important factor.

You wouldn't, for example, want to invest your cash in an offshore account in a politically unstable country, particularly if there is a risk that your assets could be expropriated.

Therefore tax planning is only one consideration. Other important factors include:

- **Privacy**. What level of disclosure is there. Will your financial affairs be kept private from prying eyes? **Ease of residence**. How easy is it to obtain permission to live in the tax haven?
- **Political stability**. Is there a risk your cash could end up in the government's coffers?
- **Communications**. How good is telephone and broadband internet access and how easy is it to travel to the country?
- **Lifestyle factors**. If you want to live there, how good is schooling, the climate, and how high is the cost of living?

It's therefore a question of what you want from your tax haven: are you only concerned with the tax position or are other factors equally important?

I mention some of these other factors elsewhere in the book, although obviously many of these are subjective and would therefore need to be addressed by you personally. We'll therefore mainly be focusing on the tax issues.

CHAPTER 1

HOW TAX HAVENS CAN HELP YOU

In this chapter we'll take a brief look at how tax havens can be used to cut your tax bill. The chapters that follow contain much more detailed information but I think it's worth explaining some of the tax planning techniques briefly before we look at some of the individual tax havens.

Most countries will tax you in one of three different ways, based on:

- **The source of your income or capital gains**. If your income is derived locally the local tax authorities will tax you on it.
- **Your country of residence**. If you are resident in a country, that country may have the right to tax you on your worldwide income or gains. The United Kingdom does this.
- **Your country of nationality.** This is rare, but is very important if it applies. Some countries such as the United States tax you if you are a national or citizen. Even if you leave the country you will still have to pay tax.

Most developed countries apply the first two rules, although the US applies all three in certain situations. It's easy to see how two countries could easily decide to tax the same income.

Example

Steve, a UK resident, has an offshore bank account in Spain. As a resident of the UK he will be liable to UK tax on his worldwide income, including his Spanish interest.

However as the interest has a Spanish source, Spain will also want to tax it. In this case the double tax treaty between the two countries would come to the rescue. Any Spanish tax paid would be allowed as a credit against Steve's UK tax liability.

What if Steve used a bank in a nil-tax haven such as the Bahamas or the Cayman Islands?

In this case there would be no overseas tax as these countries do not levy tax. However, there would still be UK taxes to pay because individuals who are UK resident and domiciled are subject to UK tax on their worldwide income.

This is crucial to understand because it dispels the myth that tax havens can be used to automatically escape taxes. Unless you are careful how you use them you will not enjoy any tax savings.

Some books hint at keeping your income private and therefore hint at tax evasion. In many countries this is the fastest way to land in jail (or at the very least end up paying substantial penalties) and I would never advise this.

You should always disclose as much information as the tax authorities in your home country require.

Every country has different disclosure requirements. For example, the US requires separate disclosure of foreign bank accounts of which you are a signatory. Other countries such as the UK do not.

It's the secrecy that European and North American tax departments don't like and this has led to growth in tax information agreements between countries and, for example, the advent of the EU Savings Tax Directive and the proposals at the April 2009 G20 summit to crack down on tax havens – we'll look at these in more detail shortly.

In terms of the EU Savings Tax Directive this is an agreement between members of the EU (and various overseas dependencies) to automatically share information with each other about customers who earn savings income in one country but live in another.

Provided you stick to these simple rules you should be able to sleep peacefully at night. And that's far more important than escaping tax!

Tax havens are useful in lots of different ways, including:

Emigration

If you fancy living abroad, one option is to live in a tax haven. Fortunately many tax havens have extremely high living standards and are beautiful places to stay. If you choose the country wisely, you may be able to completely avoid income tax and other taxes.

Emigrating to one of the nil-tax havens such as the Bahamas, St Kitts and Nevis, the Cayman Islands or the British Virgin Islands would be ideal for this purpose. US citizens cannot do this, however, because they are subject to US tax wherever they live (although there are limited tax exemptions for US citizens living abroad that can exempt the first $97,600 of earned income).

Another option may be to establish yourself in one of the foreign source exempt havens and put your money in an offshore bank account. In this way you will also not pay one penny in tax.

Finally, you could go and live in a low-tax haven if it offers concessions that suit your particular circumstances. For example, you could go and live in South Africa or New Zealand if you have a big property investment portfolio and want to escape or reduce capital gains tax.

Diverting Profits

Tax havens are often used to divert profits from a country with high tax rates to a country with low tax rates. They're also used to divert interest, royalties and management charges.

Unfortunately this is not very easy to do in practice – the country where the income is sourced is likely to have rules preventing you from doing this. However, it is possible in certain circumstances.

Example

Patrick owns a company called Compco that manufactures and sells computers. His company is located in a country with a corporation tax of 30%. Patrick decides to become non-resident and live in a tax haven, while still doing work for the company.

The advantage is that there will be no income tax to pay in the tax haven. Furthermore, provided the cost of his services is set at a reasonable commercial rate, Compco may be allowed a tax deduction for the full amount paid to Patrick. This means there will be no corporation tax on the money paid to Patrick.

Diverting income from a high-tax country to a low-tax country is one of the key benefits of using offshore tax havens.

Double Tax Treaty (DTT) Manipulation

As mentioned earlier, low-tax havens are often used to take advantage of double tax treaties. Using double tax treaties to avoid taxes can result in big savings and this makes some of the low tax destinations that have lots of double tax treaties very popular.

Example

Pedro conducts business in the United States but through an offshore company located in Cyprus.

Provided Pedro does not actually have a fixed place of business in the United States or act via an agent (the treaty defines this as having a 'permanent establishment' in the US – more on this later in the book!) the income from the business will pass to that company with little or no US tax being paid because of the tax treaty between the two countries, provided the Cyprus company is a resident of Cyprus.

If income is paid to a person or company in a jurisdiction with no tax treaty with the US, the profits will be subject to US tax, at a rate as high as 35%.

Now that the money is sitting in the Cyprus company, it could be extracted free of Cypriot taxes to a non-resident.

This example illustrates how complex offshore tax planning with tax havens can be. Everyone's situation is different, hence the need for professional advice.

Capital Gains Tax (CGT) Planning

In recent years many individuals have moved abroad to escape capital gains tax. Most are property investors who have made huge profits during the global real estate boom of recent years.

If they sold their properties without moving they'd see a large chunk of their profits going to the taxman in their country of residence or the country where the property is located.

Avoiding a big tax bill is particularly important where properties have been heavily remortgaged to enable the investor to withdraw the equity (paper profits).

Investors with large debts over some properties may actually end up with insufficient cash to cover their capital gains tax bills. Therefore they look for any opportunity, including moving overseas, to escape paying tax.

Tax havens are also used to escape CGT by entrepreneurs who've had enough of the rat race and want to sell their companies.

Using offshore company arrangements or emigrating to countries that don't charge CGT on overseas disposals can drastically reduce the tax liability.

Example

Tony, a UK resident, has a big property portfolio with profits in excess of £1 million. He wants to sell the properties and minimize the tax payable by moving offshore.

The UK doesn't currently usually impose capital gains tax on non-residents (unless they're conducting a trade from the UK) and Tony therefore decides to move to the Bahamas, sell his property portfolio and avoid paying UK capital gains tax.

The downside to this is that he would need to stay overseas for more than five complete UK tax years to avoid the gains being taxed if he returns.

Five years is too long for many people. It used to be possible to get around this by emigrating to a country with a suitable tax treaty with the UK (Greece was one such country).

Unfortunately the UK closed this loophole in the 2004 Pre Budget Report and UK emigrants are therefore usually tied in to a five year absence.

(Having said that, they could still spend a couple of months per tax year in the UK without bringing the gain back within the scope of UK taxes. The key issue here is showing that they have established their new life and home overseas.)

Inheritance Tax (IHT) Planning

If there's one tax people resent above all others it's inheritance tax. In the UK the rate of inheritance tax is 40%. Paying 40% tax on your assets is much worse than paying 40% tax on your **profits**. Furthermore, your assets will, for the most part, have been built up out of after-tax income –

meaning that they are effectively taxed twice.

The good news is there are ways that tax havens can help you reduce your inheritance tax bill. By transferring some of your wealth into an offshore trust or company you can escape the tax in certain circumstances because the trust/company becomes the new owner of the assets. Your estate will then have fewer assets to tax.

Many countries don't subject offshore trusts and companies to IHT and, if they do, it's usually an amended form of tax. Hence the correct use of offshore entities can maximize your wealth and minimize your taxes.

Once again it's important to stress that offshore tax planning is a complicated area and you should always obtain detailed professional advice from a qualified tax adviser in your country of residence. In particular, there will probably be anti-avoidance rules (most high-tax countries have them) that may apply and careful 'navigation' in these circumstances is essential.

Asset Protection

Tax havens aren't just used by people who want to pay less tax. They're also very important for the purposes of *asset protection*. You'll notice that the subtitle of this book says 'Safeguard Your Financial Freedom'.

We're not referring to saving tax here but to the importance of protecting your wealth from anyone else who may try to get their hands on it.

In recent years the UK has gone much the same way as the US and become litigation crazy.

Doctors and other professionals feel extremely vulnerable but anyone could fall victim to a frivolous lawsuit.

Others who may try to target you include ex-employees, spouses or business partners, fraudsters and other crooks, disgruntled family members or clients, ambulance-chasing lawyers and virtually anyone who knows you have money and thinks you are easy prey.

The idea of asset protection is to make your assets extremely difficult to trace and, if they are traced, extremely difficult to get hold of. For example, many tax havens have strict banking secrecy laws and as long as you are not involved in any criminal activity or money laundering your details will not be made available to third parties.

There are, of course, things you can do in your home country to protect your wealth, for example setting up a limited company or limited liability partnership.

However, many argue that nothing quite beats the privacy of setting up an offshore structure, especially if you choose a tax haven with strong privacy laws. Your creditors first have to find your offshore company, trust or bank account before they can get their hands on your money!

It's important to bear this point in mind as you read the book. You may not be able to use a tax haven to legally avoid tax... but you may be able to use one to protect your money from everyone else.

Forum Shopping

English courts have become known as a 'wives' paradise' as they favour the less wealthy spouse (still typically the wife), and it's not just wealth acquired during marriage that's at stake. English courts can also take into account wealth a spouse brought into the marriage as well as inheritances.

This is one of the reasons why 'forum shopping' is becoming so popular. Essentially it involves starting divorce proceedings in an overseas country so that the divorce is based on overseas laws. As other countries take a different view on the treatment of pre-nuptial agreements or on assets that were inherited by one of the spouses, it can lead to a reduction in the settlement.

The other reason why forum shopping is becoming important is that more and more people are marrying overseas residents or living overseas.

The G20 Crackdown on 'Tax Havens'

The G20 summit in April 2009 resulted in a number of agreements and commitments to clamp down on cross-border tax evasion. In the press it was widely reported that one of the key proposals was a clamp down on using tax havens.

This, however, does not paint the full picture. The actual report stated:

"...We call on countries to adopt the international standard for information exchange

endorsed by the G20 in 2004 and reflected in the UN Model Tax Convention. We note that the OECD has today published a list of countries assessed by the Global Forum against the international standard for exchange of information.

We welcome the new commitments made by a number of jurisdictions and encourage them to proceed swiftly with implementation.

We stand ready to take agreed action against those jurisdictions which do not meet international standards in relation to tax transparency. To this end we have agreed to develop a toolbox of effective counter measures for countries to consider, such as:

- *increased disclosure requirements on the part of taxpayers and financial institutions to report transactions involving non-cooperative jurisdictions;*
- *withholding taxes in respect of a wide variety of payments;*
- *denying deductions in respect of expense payments to payees resident in a non cooperative jurisdiction;*
- *reviewing tax treaty policy;*
- *asking international institutions and regional development banks to review their investment policies; and,*
- *giving extra weight to the principles of tax transparency and information exchange when designing bilateral aid programs..."*

What was agreed at the G20 summit is, therefore, closely tied in with the OECD Exchange of Information Treaty. The issue clearly isn't whether a country is a nil or low-tax regime – it's more an issue concerning the disclosure and exchange of information provisions countries adopt.

Essentially this report is split into three parts:

- The first list contains jurisdictions which are deemed to have 'substantially implemented' the agreed tax cooperation standard (known as the 'white list').

- The second contains the names of jurisdictions which have committed to, but have not yet implemented the standard (known as the 'grey list').

- The last list names those jurisdictions which have not committed to the standard (known as the 'black list').

Only four jurisdictions were on the 'black list' (Costa Rica, Labuan, the Philippines and Uruguay). However, since the publication of the report in 2009, these countries have all agreed to implement the proposals and are all on the 'white list'.

Since the London G20 meeting in April 2009 there has been a flurry of activity with numerous new tax information exchange agreements and double taxation conventions.

Most of the countries on the 'grey list' in 2009 (such as the Bahamas, Gibraltar and the Cayman Islands) have now moved up to the 'white list'.

This treaty requires exchange of information on request between the signatory countries. Any provisions on banking secrecy can be overridden and the country providing the information doesn't have to require the information for its own tax purposes.

It's important, however, to remember exactly what the G20 and the OECD are trying to achieve. There's nothing in all this that attempts to prevent you using a low or nil tax haven to reduce your taxes.

In fact, many of the larger developed countries that belong to the OECD and G20 themselves have tax regimes that can be used to achieve low or zero taxes. For example, in the US you have the Delaware LLC, in the UK there are special rules for non-domiciled individuals, and Spain has favourable rules for holding companies.

It's the secrecy that the OECD and G20 countries don't like and as such they're trying to ensure that there is good exchange of information between jurisdictions. It's true to a certain extent that this will affect the 'tax havens' more than other countries as they have traditionally been more reluctant to pass on information than many of the 'higher-tax' jurisdictions.

It's worthwhile bearing in mind, however, that if you were looking at using tax havens to avoid disclosing your overseas income or assets to the tax authorities in your home country, you were on very shaky ground anyway.

You should always ensure that you declare overseas income and gains to the tax authorities in your country of residence. Provided you do this, the G20 clamp down will have little impact on you.

So Who Does the Clamp Down Affect?

Anyone who holds assets or generates income in an overseas jurisdiction will potentially be affected. For example:

- Anyone with an offshore savings account
- Anyone with an offshore company
- Anyone who can benefit from an offshore trust or foundation

The G20 changes will ensure that the authorities in your home country can be passed details such as:

- Overseas account balances
- Interest earned
- Income sources and where they're generated
- Details of signatories on offshore accounts
- Company shareholders
- Beneficiaries of offshore trusts/foundations
- Settlors of offshore trusts/jurisdictions
- Company income and gains
- Trust income and gains

So long as you have accounted for these in accordance with the tax rules in your country of residence you should be OK.

Here are two examples where the G20 changes will have no impact at all:

Example 1

Jack is a UK resident and holds an interest in an offshore 'tax haven' company. The company is controlled from overseas and generates all of its income overseas. Jack isn't caught by the anti-avoidance rules because, in this case, there is no tax avoidance motive for the use of the company. In addition he has always declared this position in his self assessment tax returns. Jack is not taxed on any of the profits of the offshore company.

Example 2

Pedro is a non UK domiciliary who has been in the UK for five years. He has earned interest on an offshore savings account (located in a tax haven) and has retained the interest abroad. He has not declared the offshore interest but has declared his non UK domiciled status and now claims the remittance basis.

Because both individuals have fully complied with their UK tax obligations there will be no negative impact even if the overseas jurisdiction passes on details to the UK tax authorities.

Privacy Shopping

It's likely that most countries will implement exchange of information treaties in accordance with the OECD's recommendations. This appears to be high up on the political agenda and it's unlikely that it will lose momentum over the next year or two.

To satisfy OECD requirements (in other words to get onto the white list) a country needs to implement 12 exchange of information treaties. In Britain, the Prime Minister has however already stated that he expects British dependencies to exceed the OECD's minimum requirements.

Nevertheless, there could still be opportunities for 'privacy shopping', to avoid exchange of information requirements by choosing countries which don't have reciprocal exchange of information treaties. As stated above, however, if you are disclosing what is required this should not be necessary.

In summary, the main aim of the G20 and OECD proposals is to ensure that information is disclosed between countries. Providing you declare your overseas income and gains in accordance with the tax regime in your country of residence, these proposals should have limited impact.

They also do not prevent you from emigrating and establishing residence yourself in a low or nil tax haven.

With the UK Government getting tough on offshore evasion, as from April 2011 there will be a new penalty regime where there is a loss of tax connected with offshore activities.

The penalty regime is widely drawn up to include any loss of tax relating to income tax and capital gains tax, and is obviously aimed at UK residents trying to escape UK tax by keeping quiet about overseas income or capital gains.

As of April 2011 the penalty regime has been modified so that penalties will be increased by a factor of 1.5 if the tax loss is connected to a jurisdiction that does not exchange information with the UK automatically (as opposed to on request) and by a factor of 2 where there is no exchange of information whatsoever.

So if there is an income tax or CGT loss from a country with which the UK does not have any exchange of information treaty, the penalty will be doubled.

If there is an exchange of information treaty but it only applies to specific requests by HMRC you're looking at a penalty of 150%.

This shows the problems HMRC has in identifying taxpayers with untaxed overseas assets or income in countries where there is no automatic exchange of information.

These are, of course, maximum penalties, and can be reduced if an individual makes a prompted or unprompted disclosure.

HMRC has published a list of the countries in Category 1 and Category 3. It has not published Category 2, but says that those countries not in Category 1 or 3 will fall into Category 2.

Category 1 consists mainly of countries with automatic exchange of information with the UK. These include the Cayman Islands, Guernsey and the Isle of Man. It also includes all the EU countries, except Austria and Luxembourg.

Category 2 includes countries that exchange information with the UK on request. This includes many offshore jurisdictions.

Category 3 is mainly the territories that do not exchange information with the UK. These are listed and include Belize, Monaco and Panama.

Category 1

Anguilla	Italy
Aruba	Japan
Australia	South Korea
Belgium	Latvia
Bulgaria	Lithuania
Canada	Malta
Cayman	Montserrat
Cyprus	Netherlands
Czech Republic	New Zealand
Denmark	Norway
Estonia	Poland

Finland	Portugal
France	Romania
Germany	Slovakia
Greece	Slovenia
Guernsey	Spain
Hungary	Sweden
Ireland	United States of America
Isle of Man	

Category 3

Albania	Jamaica
Algeria	Kyrgyzstan
Andorra	Lebanon
Antigua	Macau
Armenia	Marshall Islands
Bahrain	Mauritius
Barbados	Micronesia
Belize	Monaco
Brazil	Nauru
Cameroon	Nicaragua
Cape Verde	Niue
Colombia	Palau
Congo	Panama
Cook Islands	Paraguay
Costa Rica	Peru
Curaçao	St Kitts Nevis
Cuba	Saint Lucia
North Korea	St Vincent
Dominica	San Marino
Dominican Rep	Seychelles
Ecuador	St Maarten
El Salvador	Suriname
Gabon	Syria
Grenada	Tokelau
Guatemala	Tonga
Honduras	Trinidad and Tobago
Iran	UAE
Iraq	Uruguay

CHAPTER 2

THE WORLD'S BEST TAX HAVENS

Now that we've looked at some of the ways tax havens are used it's time to take a look at the individual countries.

In the sections that follow we'll be looking at the following countries:

- Andorra
- Anguilla
- The Bahamas
- Barbados
- Belize
- Bermuda
- The British Virgin Islands (BVI)
- Campione
- The Cayman Islands
- The Channel Islands
- The Cook Islands
- Costa Rica
- Cyprus
- Dubai
- Eastern Europe
- Gibraltar
- Hong Kong
- Ireland
- Isle of Man
- Liechtenstein
- Malta
- Monaco
- Panama
- Seychelles
- Singapore
- St Kitts and Nevis
- Switzerland
- Turks and Caicos Islands (TCI)

We'll also be exploring a few of the 'alternative' tax havens.

ANDORRA

If you want to live in a European tax haven, you should certainly put Andorra on your shopping list. Andorra has no income tax or inheritance tax and is very popular with retirees.

There is, however, a capital gains tax on Andorran property. This is levied at 15%, reduced by 1% per year of residence. Employees pay national insurance contributions and there are some limited municipal property taxes.

Andorran companies are subject to a corporation tax charge of 10%.

There is no personal income tax for 2014 but there are proposals to bring in income tax from 2015.

Changes from 2015

From 1 January 2015, Andorra will levy both Income tax and CGT.

Income tax will be charged at a maximum rate of 10%.

For earned income (which includes salary, pension income, consultancy fees and rental income) earned both in Andorra and overseas tax will be charged on individuals as follows:

- Income of up to 23.999€ per annum - exempt.
- Income between 24.000€ and 39.999€ at 5%
- Income above 40.000€ at 10% thereafter

Married or legal couples will pay tax at the following rate:

- Income of up to 40.000€ per annum - exempt
- Income above 40.000€ per annum at 10% thereafter.

Dividend income, and interest from bonds, bank deposits or loans, will be taxed at 10% on amounts above 3.000€.

There are also proposals to introduce CGT at 10%.

However, foreign tax will be deducted from any Andorran tax.

Even with these changes, for many expats the tax payable, particularly if they derive income from overseas, will be minimal.

Work permits are notoriously difficult to get. They are usually only issued to EU nationals and then only if there is no Andorran who is qualified to do the job. Work permits are given only to individuals working for an Andorran person or company and are not given to self-employed foreigners.

Andorra has recently introduced changes to their residency requirement and have introduced new categories of residence.

Histrorically most tax exiles would seek to acquire a Passive Residence Permit. Although this does not allow you to obtain employment in Andorra or run an Andorran business (i.e. with Andorran employees and commercial premises) you could still, for example, run an internet business out of the principality or a consultancy business with clients in other countries.

To qualify for a Passive Residence Permit you are expected to live in the principality for more than 90 days per year... but this rule is not policed and is seemingly irrelevant.

New categories of residence include a new company option which involves paying a bond of €50,000 and forming an Andorran company.

Andorra is a tiny country (less than 35 miles long) and some residents complain that it is a little claustrophobic. There is a relatively small expat community. So if you only speak English the social scene may be somewhat limited.

However, the country is blessed with beautiful scenery and is a mecca for tourists in both summer and winter.

Many residents have properties in France or Spain that they escape to at the weekend. As a result, the roads are often congested at these times. However, lots of the upper valleys are quiet, very beautiful and a walker's and skier's paradise.

The climate is excellent with lots of winter (and summer) sunshine and is surprisingly dry. People with chest complaints go there for health reasons.

On the downside, as it is located in the Pyrenees, Andorra doesn't have its own international airport. The nearest ones are Toulouse and Barcelona, 3½ hours and 2½ hours away by road respectively.

Andorra seems to avoid much of the barmy EU regulation and red tape by hiding away in the mountains.

From a tax perspective, it is certainly attractive, in particular for Europeans not wanting to move too far from home.

In addition, as a place to squirrel away your savings, Andorra is hard to beat. There are no exchange controls and the banks also offer numbered accounts (accounts that have no name and just a number).

The country does, however, have some strict anti-money-laundering legislation aimed at criminals, although this excludes tax evasion, which is not a crime in Andorra.

Andorra has also signed up to the OECD Exchange of Information Treaty and is on the OECD white list having signed over 12 tax information exchange agreements.

Most expatriates who go to live in Andorra for tax reasons end up in the La Massna or Ordino parishes, where property prices are higher than elsewhere.

Property in Andorra rose by about 10% per year for many years but it is still dirt cheap compared with other European tax havens such as Monaco.

In recent times some sellers have had to reduce their asking prices to attract buyers, so it may be possible to obtain a discount if you negotiate carefully.

One-bedroom apartments cost from €125,000 (with some studio flats going for as little as €75,000) and two bedrooms from €175,000. However, at these prices you really are scraping the bottom of the barrel. The finish on the properties looks distinctly average and the locations appear undeveloped.

A half-decent two-bedroom apartment with a reasonable view will cost around €225,000. But two bedrooms in the best location with a large terrace and superb view will cost around €380,000.

The best properties will usually include basement parking (essential in winter) and be finished to a high standard. A good view or garden would add considerably to the price.

Unlike in many tax havens, detached houses are reasonably affordable. A four-bedroom or five-bedroom chalet can be yours for between €900,000 and €2 million (although the cheapest houses are tiny). Semi-detached houses and duplexes can be had for less.

There is a tax of around 2.5% on property transfers and estate agent commission is extortionate, ranging from 5% to 10%.

Renting may be an attractive alternative to buying because rents are quite low relative to property prices, especially in the countryside. Furthermore, you don't have to buy a property to obtain a Residence Permit.

Obtaining a Residence Permit doesn't seem to be all that difficult, provided you can fulfil the various criteria. It's probably worth employing the services of an experienced agent who can guide you through the bureaucracy and form filling, however.

For the passive residence permit the requirements have been tightened up and there is a requirement to pay a bond of €50,000 to the Government, plus €10,000 each for every other household member. This is fully refundable when you leave the country but you will not receive any interest on the money.

It is also necessary to show that you have funds available in a local Andorran bank equivalent to three times the national minimum wage (approximately €33,000 plus €11,000 for each additional household member).

A total of €400,000 needs to be invested in Andorra to obtain the passive residence permit.

You do not have to prove that you have a continual annual income and apparently you can use the above funds to pay the €50,000 bond.

You must also arrange private health insurance. Apparently this can be arranged, without a medical check, for less than €1,000 per person. You also have to obtain a medical certificate (apparently just an interview with a doctor at Immigration).

Residence permits are issued for a period of one year, renewable for a period of three years.

All in all, Andorra is one of the top European tax havens, particularly for UK residents not wanting to move too far. The Passive Residence scheme is highly attractive and can allow expats to live in Andorra effectively free of direct taxes.

There is a low VAT rate which is 4.5%.

ANGUILLA

Most people have never heard of Anguilla. It's a British overseas territory in the north-eastern Caribbean and is only 16 miles long.

If beaches are your thing, this place will be right up your street – it has over 30 of them. And as you'd expect it's pretty hot with an average temperature of 80 degrees, and low rainfall.

To top it all, Anguilla also has some of the most reasonably priced property in the Caribbean. Beautiful properties can be snapped up for a fraction of the price you would pay on one of the better-known Caribbean islands.

As for tax, Anguilla is about as good as it gets. It's one of the nil-tax havens, which means there is no:

- Income tax
- Inheritance or other estate taxes
- Capital gains tax
- Gift tax, or
- Corporation tax

So if you're thinking about moving overseas and living off your investments, you could enjoy a totally tax-free lifestyle if you based yourself there. There is a limited tax on local property (like many countries) but the Government has repeatedly stated that it is committed to preserving Anguilla as a key 'offshore centre' (in other words low or nil taxes!).

Anguilla is also a popular location for trusts, in particular Asset Protection Trusts (APTs). This type of trust is often set up by wealthy doctors, lawyers and dentists who want to protect their assets from negligence claims or anyone else who wants to protect their assets from spurious lawsuits and the like.

Anguilla is one of the top jurisdictions for such trusts, mainly because of its strict privacy laws. The courts in Anguilla only allow very restricted claims against trusts if the claim relates to divorce, debts or overseas taxes.

Anguilla has very few double tax treaties but it does have excellent banks and financial services. There are well over 100 banks there, including such prestigious names as Barclays and Bank of America.

The fact that it is a British dependency also adds comfort to some, as this reduces the likelihood of any civil unrest, given the protection promised by the British Government.

If you're moving to Anguilla from one of the more developed countries, such as the United Kingdom or the USA, one of the big attractions may also be the low crime rate.

Although property prices are quite reasonable in some areas, they have shot up since we first started publishing this guide, as more and more people have cottoned on to the fact that the island has a high standard of living as well as being one of the best tax havens around.

The best oceanfront homes or ones with superb ocean views go for between $800,000 and $3.5 million. An oceanfront condominium can be picked up for around $350,000.

As a non-Anguillan, bear in mind that you will have to pay an additional 12.5% Alien Land Holding License, in addition to a 5% transfer tax (this is one of the ways the government raises revenue without charging taxes on income).

Furthermore, there are restrictions on the *type* of property you can buy. In particular, beachfront homes cannot be bought by foreigners but you can buy oceanfront or rocky-coastline properties.

Obtaining residence in Anguilla is not easy and, unlike other Caribbean jurisdictions, there is no minimum number of days you have to spend there in order to be classed as a resident.

If you want to work on the island you need to obtain a work permit and, as with most Caribbean destinations, the authorities are reluctant to issue one if they think you'll be taking jobs away from locals (although if you're working in a specialised field a more relaxed attitude will be taken).

If you want to obtain permanent residence you'll need to buy a property and apply for a permanent residence certificate. This will allow easier exit and entry through Customs when you leave Anguilla but could also be shown to overseas tax authorities to back up your claim to being resident abroad.

Given the fact that Anguilla is becoming a popular tax haven, obtaining local tax advice is not difficult. You'll find some of the world's biggest law and accounting firms have offices on the island (although be prepared to pay at least $500-$750 per hour for tax-planning services).

If you're looking for an offshore company located in a tax-free jurisdiction, Anguilla offers an International Business Company (IBC), which allows trading outside Anguilla free of Anguillan tax. Not a good choice as a holding company, however, as there are few double tax treaties but it can be a useful type of company if you're looking for local tax and asset protection.

It should be noted, though, that Anguilla is subject to the EU Savings directive (See Chapter 9) and therefore EU residents will be subject to the exchange of information provisions with their home country.

In addition, Anguilla has agreed to implement the OECD Exchange of Information Treaty and is now on the OECD white list.

THE BAHAMAS

The Bahamas is made up of about 700 islands and 2,500 cays that are spread over 750 miles of the Atlantic Ocean. Only a few of these islands are actually inhabited.

The Bahamas is one of the top Caribbean tax havens and, like Anguilla, is a nil-tax haven. So there is no:

- Income tax
- Corporation tax
- Capital gains tax
- Inheritance tax

Lots of countries class themselves as having low taxation. However, the Bahamas truly is a zero-tax jurisdiction and it doesn't even levy any sales taxes. And this favourable state of affairs applies to everyone, including companies and trusts.

There are excellent travel links and the airport has half a dozen daily flights to Miami and other major destinations such as London and New York.

For US residents, the Bahamas is particularly attractive because it's the closest tax haven to the United States. It can take as little as 45 minutes to fly from Florida to Nassau.

If you're thinking of moving to the Bahamas you can expect plenty of sun and an outdoor lifestyle. Activities such as tennis, scuba diving, golf, snorkelling, fishing and cricket are all popular.

Escaping crime is a key factor for many emigrants and while the Bahamas has a relatively low crime rate, it can still be an issue, especially in Nassau, where there is significant drug-related crime.

The Sting in the Tail – Import Duties

Although the Bahamas has practically no taxation, the Government still needs to raise revenue from somewhere. It does this by charging company licence fees, social security on workers, stamp duty, property taxes and, worst of all, sky-high import duties.

Import duties average 35%, so if you're planning on living in the Bahamas, the main issue is likely to be the high cost of living.

As always it will depend on the lifestyle that you choose. If you expect to live in the same way as you did in the UK or US and eat similar foods etc, you will end up paying through the nose for imported products. If you adapt and eat local produce, it will cost less.

There is no escaping the fact that the Bahamas is an expensive place to live. For example, rents are pretty steep and upmarket three-bedroom condos and houses around Nassau cost around $5,000 per month.

However, some of these properties have truly stunning ocean views and their own swimming pools.

A few rungs down the ladder you will find two-bedroom cottages with nice little gardens going for $2,500 to $3,000 per month in the Sandyport gated community near Nassau.

Dubbed the Venice of the Bahamas, this development contains over 300 homes built around picturesque canals. The properties have 24-hour security, shared swimming pools, tennis courts and other facilities.

Nearby on Paradise Island you can find two-bedroom condos with shared pools and gardens and easy access to beaches for just $2,500 per month.
For $3,500 per month you can rent a two-bedroom oceanfront penthouse near Cable Beach, complete with a large balcony looking over the sea, with a gym and shared pool.

For $3,800 you can have a three-bedroom villa with a private pool on Paradise Island in a gated community with 24-hour security.

There are cheaper properties available to rent for around $1,000 per month. For example, in Freeport on Grand Bahama I have seen a two-bedroom condo with a beautiful view of the canal for just $900 per month.

The Bahamas is one of the most popular of the Caribbean tax havens. The banking sector is huge and has acquired an excellent reputation as a location for offshore banking.

However, it's fair to say that its appeal has weakened somewhat among US residents following the signing of a tax information and exchange agreement with the American Government.

Nevertheless, the Bahamas still offers excellent confidentiality to residents of other countries.

The IEA allows the US Internal Revenue Service to obtain details of offshore accounts held by US residents and effectively overrules the strict banking secrecy usually in place in the Bahamas.

Note that many of the 'larger' tax havens have signed the IEA as well, including the Cayman Islands, Bermuda and Jersey.

The Bahamas has also agreed to implement the OECD Exchange of Information Treaty and has now moved off the OECD grey list on to the white list as it has now signed over 12 tax information exchange agreements.

Becoming Resident in the Bahamas

It is possible to obtain annual or permanent residence in the Bahamas. Your application will be treated more favourably if you own a residence worth more than $500,000. Some say this will result in almost automatic approval.

Generally, local jobs are not open to foreigners, unless you have a particular skill that is not available on the islands.

With the advent of the internet, many people looking to emigrate also plan to work remotely. If you are 'telecommuting' you will not need a work permit as your business will not be trading in the Bahamas and your income will come from overseas.

An annual residence permit is available as an independent economic resident for $1,000 per year with a financial reference from a reputable bank that verifies your economic worth and two character references.

You can also obtain an annual homeowner's residence card that is renewable annually for $500 and allows you and your family to stay for up to one year.

You can also apply for permanent residence on economic grounds because you invest or own a home in the Bahamas.

Buying Property

Cheap properties are available, with studio apartments starting at as little as $150,000. Two-bedroom condominiums can be found for $250,000.

However, if you want to buy a property for more than $500,000 to help with a residence application, there are some fabulous homes priced at between $500,000 and $750,000.

For example in the Treasure Cove gated community near Nassau you can find a lovely three-bedroom house with its own pool for $520,000.

In the residential resort of Treasure Cay on Abaco there are two-bedroom houses right on the beach for $570,000.

For $689,000 you can find two-bedroom apartments in a gated complex in Cable Beach near Nassau with a huge covered porch, spectacular ocean views, a shared pool and easy access to the beach.

If you climb a few rungs up the property ladder, there are no end of simply amazing waterfront three- and four-bedroom houses for over $1 million dotted around the various islands.

Offshore Companies

Just as in Anguilla, if you're looking for a tax-free offshore company, a Bahamian International Business Company (IBC) may be just what you're looking for. With traditionally good financial privacy, the Bahamas is a popular location for non-resident companies.

BARBADOS

Barbados is firmly in the 'low tax' or, more accurately, 'some tax' category. There is no:

- Capital gains tax, or
- Inheritance tax and gift tax.

However, the authorities do levy income tax and VAT (mostly at 17.5%).

To a certain extent there is a trade-off because, if you want to live in a well-developed country with a good telephone network, a relatively good road and transportation network and good schools you're going to have to pay some tax.

Income tax in Barbados is not low by tax haven standards. The rate for 2014 is 17.5% on income up to BDS$35,000 and 35% on income over BDS$35,000. (US$1 dollar = BDS$2.)

There is a basic deduction (personal allowance) of BDS$25,000. Those over 60 years of age and in receipt of a pension are entitled to a basic deduction of BDS$40,000.

Some people could end up paying more or less the same amount of income tax in Barbados as they would in the US or UK. So why would anyone bother moving to Barbados to escape tax?

Aside from the fact that there is no capital gains tax or inheritance tax, if you are resident but *non-domiciled* in Barbados you will only be taxed on overseas income that you actually bring into the country.

This means an emigrant can often completely avoid income tax by keeping income out of Barbados.

Furthermore, qualified expats working in the international business and financial sector can qualify for a tax exemption for 35% of their income, for the first three years.

If you want to work in Barbados you will have to pay national insurance contributions. Again these are quite high for a tax haven: 10.1% paid by the employee and 11.25% paid by the employer. For self-employed persons, the rate is 16.1%.

However, national insurance is only payable on up to BDS$4,180 per month of earnings.

National insurance is of no concern to retirees and others who intend to live off investment income. However, if you are thinking about setting up a business offshore and possibly employing staff, national insurance and other types of social security are an additional cost that you need to be aware of.

Barbados also has a property transfer tax that is paid by the person *selling* the property. The tax is set at 2.5% on the amount in excess of BDS$150,000. There is also stamp duty of 1%.

Prior to April 2007 property transfer tax was levied at 7.5% and it was quite common for foreigners to purchase properties via offshore companies to avoid it. This tax-planning technique is less popular now that the tax rate has been reduced to just 2.5%.

There is also an annual land tax that property owners have to pay at the following rates:

First BDS$150,000	0%
Next BDS$250,000	0.1%
Next BDS$600,000	0.45%
Over BDS$1 million	0.75%

For example, if you own a house worth US$500,000 (BDS$1 million) you would have to pay annual land tax of US$1,475. Pensioners enjoy a 50% discount.

Unlike the nil-tax havens, Barbados currently has over 20 double tax treaties. However, that's not very many compared with some of the other low tax havens, such as Cyprus and Gibraltar.

The treaties provide for low withholding taxes on dividends and royalties paid from countries such as Malta, Norway, the US and the UK. There is also an exchange of information agreement with the US.

The US-Barbados double tax treaty has been used by many to hold US real estate and avoid US estate taxes. Essentially, non-Barbadian individuals have set up Barbados International Business Companies and these companies have held shares in US real estate companies.

It may then be possible to live in a third country, such as the UK, and use the Barbadian tax treaty to obtain these tax benefits. Note that you would then need to consider your home country's tax rules (for example, the UK would then bring the US property into your estate if you were resident/domiciled in the UK).

Corporate Taxation

Corporation tax in Barbados is high. The basic rate is 25% and the rate for approved small businesses is 15%.

To qualify for the lower tax rate the business must generally have:

- BDS$1 million or less of paid up capital
- Turnover must not exceed BDS$2 million
- 25 or fewer employees

Unless there are special reasons for using a Barbadian company (for example, tax treaty benefits) these would not be at the top of most lists.

The concept of 'domicile' applies to companies as well as individuals, so a company resident in Barbados but incorporated elsewhere is taxed on its foreign income on a remittance basis.

If you do want to incorporate a company in Barbados, you would be better off looking at a Barbadian IBC. There's a special IBC regime, which is used mainly by offshore trading companies (note, not investment companies) that allows a reduced rate of corporation tax payable, often as low as 1% to 2.5%.

Who Can Use Barbados to Save Tax?

Although the income tax is punitive, especially when compared with other offshore centres, in practice someone becoming resident in Barbados can easily make use of their non-domiciled status to protect overseas income from tax.

In terms of residence, the traditional definition applies with an individual becoming Barbadian resident for the whole year after spending more than 182 days there during a calendar year (which in Barbados is the same as the tax year).

Added to this is the fact that there is no capital gains tax, making Barbados a useful jurisdiction for individuals who want to cut their CGT bills when disposing of overseas assets. It also has some limited double tax treaties in place that could be effective in reducing withholding taxes.

Celebrity Spotting

If you want to mingle with the rich and famous, Barbados is likely to be right up your street, as many celebrities either visit or have properties there.

It's known as a wealthy, well-developed island (it has one of the highest literacy rates in the world – 98%) and unlike some of the other tax haven islands, you'll see plenty of expensive cars if you visit (Jaguars, BMWs and Mercedes).

The cost of living is very high, so don't consider moving there unless you have a lot of disposable income. But on the plus side, there are plenty of luxury properties available, the beaches are superb and crime is pretty low (except for burglary). All in all, Barbados offers a very high standard of living, but at a price.

Buying a Home in Barbados

If you're considering buying a home in Barbados, property is available to non-Barbadians without any major restrictions (no need to get a licence as in Anguilla).

Property prices tend to be higher than in the British Virgin Islands but not as high as Bermuda.

At the luxury end you can pick up a beautiful four-bedroom house right on the beach for around £2.5 million.

There are, however, some fantastic houses, condominiums and apartments with sea views and pools, priced at between £400,000 and £1 million.

There are also many properties that cost less than £300,000 but you will have to search hard for one with any 'wow factor'. It is possible to buy one-bedroom studio apartments for as little as £100,000.

Estate agents' commission is 5% for sellers.

BELIZE

Belize is an independent country close to Mexico. Just like Barbados there is no capital gains tax or inheritance tax but there is income tax fixed at the flat rate of 25%. If you are an employee, there are social security contributions on top of that.

Belize also has a special tax rule for individuals who are resident but not domiciled there: you only pay tax on income derived in Belize. This, therefore, exempts from tax most immigrants, who usually keep their money invested offshore.

It's mainly individuals actually working in Belize who end up paying income tax.

Of course, it's not just the tax environment that needs to be considered. You would also need to consider whether Belize is the kind of place you would want to live. As far as tax havens go, it's undoubtedly one of the least developed and should only really be considered if you want a quiet life in a quiet backwater. The standard of living is relatively low and you'll be hard pushed to find a McDonald's or Burger King!

You can get your favourite western products but you'll pay through the nose for them.

Many of the properties on offer look a bit over-priced for what they are (pretty basic), although the locations can be impressive. In many cases the properties are more vacation homes than anything else. Oceanfront homes start at around US$400,000. There are numerous lots of land for sale.

Stamp duty is 5%, with the first $10,000 exempt, although non-residents and those who have only been resident for a short period pay an additional 10%.

Given its reputation as a drug-trafficking centre, Belize is not usually thought of as the place to go if you want to escape crime. However, the country does have pretty stiff anti-drug laws and the problem tends to be confined to the major cities.

Local Belize companies pay corporation tax at the rate of 25%. However, if you're thinking about using an offshore entity you wouldn't be using a 'standard' Belizean company. Instead you would be using a Belizean international business company (IBC). This is exempt from all forms of tax in Belize.

It's not an ideal place for an offshore holding company due to the lack of double tax treaties with other countries (there are only treaties with the UK, Sweden, Denmark, some Caribbean countries and Austria) and is often used by offshore nominee or recharging companies.

How to Get a Residence Permit

One of the benefits of Belize is that it has pretty lax residence requirements and there are some established programmes that effectively let you buy your way in.

There is also a special Qualified Retired Persons programme for retirees, in terms of which you can get permanent residence provided you are aged at least 45, can support yourself by earning at least US$2,000 per month (just US$2,000 for couples), and spend at least part of the year in Belize. The Belize authorities have recently confirmed that this scheme will continue despite contrary reports in the press.

Of course the aim behind this scheme is to encourage foreigners to bring in their cash to boost the local economy and from the immigrant's perspective, taking into account the low property prices and the low income threshold, it does offer an excellent opportunity to establish a tax haven lifestyle at minimal initial cost.

You can also establish residence by becoming a regular permanent resident. To qualify, you don't have to deposit a sum with the central bank but, as expected, you must prove that you have sufficient financial resources to support yourself and your family.

BERMUDA

Everyone knows that Bermuda is a beautiful place. However, it's also attractive from a tax perspective. There is no:

- Income tax
- Capital gains tax
- VAT

There is a payroll tax that is levied on employers. The tax is currently as much as 14% and the employer can recover 5.25% from the employee.

A major source of tax is customs duty, levied on almost all goods arriving on the island (including a 25% tax on your belongings if you emigrate there).

If you own property in Bermuda you will be subject to an annual land tax. This tax is based on the annual rental value of the property. The rates range from 0.6% to 19.2%. Pensioners who are 65 or older are exempt.

There is also stamp duty on estates, which will be payable if you own assets in Bermuda on your date of death. The rates vary from 5% (BMD100,001 to BMD200,000) to 20% (assets in excess of BMD 2 million).

Living in Bermuda

Bermuda appeals to wealthy British expats because of the strong British culture and the mild subtropical climate. The island is also famous for its pink beaches.

Crime is certainly lower than in most of the US or Europe but is growing, particularly in the back streets of the capital.

Bermuda is one of the most affluent countries in the world and the cost of living is one of the highest in the world.

If you wish to live there you will have to apply for a Residential Certificate. To obtain one you generally have to own a property and be retired (over 50 years of age with substantial financial means).

Buying Property in Bermuda

Non-Bermudians can only buy higher-priced properties that are already foreign owned.

You have to obtain a licence from the Minister for Labour, Home Affairs and Public Safety.

The licence fee is currently 25% of the purchase price for a house but only 6.5% or 18% for a condominium.

You can only acquire a house that has an annual rentable value (ARV) of at least $153,000 or a condominium with an ARV of $32,500 or more, located in "designated development".

The ARV is set by the land valuation office and is not necessarily a true reflection of the rent that could be achieved on the open market.

If you wish to rent out the property, you have to apply for permission from the minister and this is seldom granted for more than 12 months.

The sale of undeveloped residential land to non-Bermudians is generally prohibited.

Realistically, if it's a family home you are after, you would be looking at paying over US$5 million. The largest selection of properties in this price bracket is located in the Tuckers Town, Point Shares, Harbour Road and the South Shore areas.

Setting Up an Offshore Company in Bermuda

Bermuda has a massive slice of the offshore company market (it has over 12,000 international companies) and some of the big FTSE and Fortune 100 companies have offshore holding companies incorporated on the island.

Bermuda is particularly popular with US companies given its geographic location. However, of more importance is the fact that it offers tax exemptions to companies incorporated under special exempt and overseas company provisions.

Bermuda is also a pretty well developed country with excellent communications and professional services and offers political stability.

One of the main reasons for the number of offshore companies in Bermuda has been the captive insurance regulations. Essentially, captive insurance allows companies to 'self-insure' their own liabilities. It has also been a popular tax-planning device, allowing a tax deduction for insurance premiums and a roll-up of cash tax free in Bermuda. However, the IRS has closed many of these loopholes.

Note that, like the Bahamas, Bermuda has signed an information exchange agreement with the US and therefore any US citizens could find the IRS obtaining info on any interest earned from a Bermuda bank account.

It has also implemented the terms of the OECD Exchange of Information Treaty and is now on the OECD white list, having implemented more than 30 exchange of information treaties.

Note that a plus for Bermuda at the moment is that it is excluded from the impact of the EU Savings Tax Directive, although the Bermuda authorities are in discussions with the EU regarding this.

THE BRITISH VIRGIN ISLANDS (BVI)

The British Virgin Islands is one of the most famous tax havens, thanks to being featured in numerous novels and films. This is also where you'll find Richard Branson's very own Necker Island.

In the British Virgin Islands there is no:

- Capital gains tax
- Income tax
- Corporation tax
- Inheritance tax
- Sales tax

The BVI has signed an exchange of information agreement with the UK and is on the OECD's white list, having signed more than 17 exchange of information treaties.

Only individuals employed in the BVI and businesses operating there pay any taxes.

The main taxes are payroll tax and social security tax.

Payroll tax is generally levied at 14%. Small businesses with turnover of US$300,000 or less, seven or fewer employees and payrolls not exceeding $150,000, are liable to payroll tax at 10%.

The employer can opt to deduct 8% from the employee in each case. The first $10,000 is tax free for both the employee and employer.

With social security tax, 4% is paid by the employee and 4½% by the employer on earnings up to $36,200.

These taxes would only be payable if you are working in the BVI.

So if you use a BVI company as an overseas investment company or for recharging, there could well be no tax payable in the British Virgin Islands.

The BVI uses the same rules as the UK to decide if a company is resident in the BVI or not. Any company that is incorporated there or is managed and controlled from there is treated as BVI resident.

The BVI is a popular choice for establishing offshore companies (usually IBCs). It has a number of advantages including:

- Easy access to and from the islands from North America and Europe. Telephone, internet and postal services are good (as you would expect from one of the main offshore financial centres).
- The official language is English.
- The BVI has traditionally offered excellent privacy as IBCs can offer bearer shares.

Bearer shares allow you to keep details of your shareholding private as ownership of the shares passes simply by physical transfer.

Note that the BVI has now made changes to the bearer share regime so that the name of the beneficial owner would need to be provided to certain 'custodians', such as certain financial institutions, who would have to guarantee confidentiality. Therefore, whilst still allowing bearer shares, the privacy benefits have been diluted somewhat.

Overall, the British Virgin Islands are an excellent base for establishing an offshore company and its use as a corporate tax haven is undoubtedly growing.

Buying a Property in the BVI

Stamp duty is levied at 12% on property transactions and Building Tax is levied at 1.5% of the annual rental value.

Accommodation is of good quality and generally cheaper than the Cayman Islands and Bermuda.

£200,000 will buy you a two-bedroom apartment in a condominium village on Virgin Gorda with a shared pool.

£500,000 will buy you a two-bedroom house with stunning ocean views on Tortola, the largest and most populated of the British Virgin Islands.
Before you can buy property in the BVI you will need to obtain permission from the BVI authorities (known as a Non-Belongers Land Holding Licence).

Living in the BVI

The cost of living is high but less than Bermuda and slightly less than the Caymans (much the same as the UK, in fact). Crucially, crime is very low.

If you are looking to move permanently to the BVI there are no special residency or citizenship programmes.

You could obtain residency by investing significant sums in the local economy or by marrying a local! There is no minimum investment stipulated and this would be a matter of negotiation with the BVI authorities.

CAMPIONE

Campione is more accurately known as 'Campione d'Italia' because it is a small sovereign Italian territory albeit completely surrounded by Swiss territory.

It's often described as an Italian enclave on Swiss territory. This means that for all intents and purposes you're living in Switzerland on a day-to-day basis. So it has a Swiss customs regime, Swiss currency and stamps.
Campione residents use Swiss telephone companies but the electricity comes directly from Italy (but is paid for in Swiss francs!). Local employees have their salaries paid in Swiss francs and they use a favourable exchange rate, much less than the market rate.

Campione is a tiny province with around 3,000 inhabitants. It has been touted as a tax haven in the past but with the reduction in revenues from the casinos over the last few years, taxes have been more rigorously collected by the tax authorities.

Taxes in Campione

Although you are actually living on Swiss territory, Campione belongs to Italy.

As such, residents of Campione are subject to Italian taxes. Italian taxes are traditionally high but there is some respite as residents of Campione don't pay full Italian income tax. Based on a special provision in the Italian law, the first CHF 200,000 income is exchanged into Euros, the official currency in Italy, at a special exchange rate.

This results in a lower effective income and consequently a lower tax rate. This, however, only applies to the first CHF 200,000 of income. Aside from this special concession the normal Italian tax laws and tax rates apply.

So if you pay tax at the highest rate you'll be facing a 43% Italian income tax rate. If your income is less than around £133,000 (roughly equivalent to CHF 200,000) you will be able to take advantage of the special exchange rate provisions.

The Special Exchange Rate

Essentially, residents of Campione can invoice their services in Swiss Francs. For tax purposes they also benefit from a formal facilitated exchange rate that is set every three years through a Ministerial Decree (eg 1 CHF = 0.40482 Euro).

Income tax returns are prepared by converting the declared Swiss Francs into Euros using this exchange rate and then paying the taxes due in Euros, resulting in potentially significant tax savings.

As for 'normal' Italian residents, there are no inheritance and gift taxes and income from interest on foreign bonds paid through an Italian bank is taxed at a special reduced rate of only 12.5%.

The other advantage is that there is no Italian VAT charged. Campione is considered to be outside the EU for tax purposes. Therefore, exports to Campione and services performed by residents of Campione are outside the scope of VAT and, therefore, invoiced without VAT.

There's little doubt that Campione is a very scenic location but if you're predominantly concerned with reducing or avoiding taxes, it's difficult to see how it could be high up on anyone's list.

Certainly when compared with the traditional tax havens such as Monaco and Andorra, there is no real competition.

Even when compared with the low tax havens such as Cyprus, Malta, Bulgaria and the Isle of Man, Campione falls short of the mark. You also need to bear in mind the very high cost of acquiring residence there.

Although there's no formal residence scheme you would need to acquire property. Given the very high demand for property, you would be lucky to find anything for under £500,000.

Although it's not in the same price league as Monaco, it doesn't offer the tax-free status that Monaco does.

THE CAYMAN ISLANDS

The Cayman Islands are one of the most famous tax havens and are a Hollywood favourite (this is where the Tom Cruise movie The Firm was filmed).

Located in the Caribbean, they're an English-speaking dependent territory of the United Kingdom.

The Cayman Islands give the impression of being a great hideaway where the rich and famous stash their millions free of tax. But just how true is this?

Well, the Caymans certainly appear to offer the traditional benefits of a tax haven since they currently have no:

- Income tax
- Corporation tax
- Capital gains tax
- Inheritance tax or other estate taxes

The Government raises its revenue from customs duties, stamp duty and annual company fees.

The Caymans have a number of advantages that have helped establish its reputation as an offshore centre, including:

- Excellent political stability
- No exchange control - funds can be moved freely in or out
- Traditionally watertight confidentiality laws (although these have now been slightly eroded)
- Close proximity to the US
- Excellent communications
- Sophisticated legal, accounting and banking services

The Cayman Islands' position as one of the world's top tax havens is supported by the fact that it is the largest offshore banking centre in the world with over 600 banks. It is also home to some big trust businesses.

The Cayman Islands allow you to set up exempt companies that are entitled to receive a 'Tax Exemption Undertaking' – a tax-free guarantee from the

Government for up to 30 years (20 years initially but renewable for a further 10 years). This will protect you in the event that taxes are ever introduced in the Cayman Islands. The company is not allowed to conduct business inside the Cayman Islands.

It is also possible to set up exempt limited partnerships that qualify for a 50-year exemption from any Cayman Islands tax (should any be introduced in the future).

Cayman exempt companies are viewed by many advisers as being some of the most flexible types of offshore companies available. Reporting requirements are minimal (essentially just a signed statement) and companies can be incorporated within 24 hours. The names of shareholders do not have to be filed with the Registrar of Companies.

Cayman Islands exempt companies are also allowed to issue bearer shares and use nominee shareholders. This allows holdings in Cayman companies to be kept private. Nominee shareholders, in particular, are intended to disguise the true ownership of a company. (Many professional advisers do not recommend bearer shares because of the inherent security risks.)

It will generally cost you more to incorporate an IBC in the Cayman Islands than in certain other jurisdictions such as Costa Rica, St Kitts Nevis or Mauritius.

The minimum government registration fee is US$732 per year. However, this is likely to be the least of your costs. You will probably pay at least US$2,500 (possibly US$4,000 or more) to form a Cayman IBC, whereas a Costa Rican IBC can be set up for less than US$1,000.

Offshore Companies – General Tip

It's important to point out that there are lots of internet services that will set you up with an offshore company for a nominal fee.

This doesn't necessarily mean that you will end up with a company that is fit for purpose. It is also essential to consult a local tax specialist, in your own jurisdiction, to ensure that your ideas are valid.

You also have to be aware of fees for optional services and ongoing services.

For example, setting up a business bank account could cost another $1,000.

One firm that sets up companies on the Isle of Man will provide a nominee director and secretary (so that the client's name does not appear on any corporate documents) for a cost of £1,000 per year.

In the Cayman Islands it is a statutory requirement that every company has a registered office on the Cayman Islands. Registered office services cost around $1,000 per year. Mail forwarding and other secretarial services could add another $1,000 per year. Specialist tax/legal advice will probably cost at least $500 per hour.

The Asian Connection

Cayman Islands companies are particularly popular with US businesses looking to trade in China for both tax-planning purposes and providing a suitable exit strategy.

The Cayman Islands is one of only a handful of jurisdictions whose companies can obtain a listing on the Hong Kong Stock Exchange.

Confidentiality

The Caymans were traditionally well known for their confidentiality.
A potential blot on the landscape is the Information Exchange Agreement (IEA) signed with the US. The agreement specifies that the Cayman Islands will share information with the US Government to help it trace financial criminals.

In addition, the Cayman Islands also implement the EU Savings Tax Directive and the OECD Exchange of Information Treaty, as well as agreeing to exchange information on an ad hoc basis with numerous other countries.

This certainly dents the Caymans' reputation for secrecy. Under the IEA with the US, for instance, provided the US Government has a suspicion that an offence has been committed, it can request access to Cayman bank accounts.

In December 2010 a Double Taxation Arrangement between the UK and the Cayman Islands came into force. This provides for the exchange of tax information between the two countries. The Cayman Islands has therefore effectively ripped up its previous policy of non-disclosure and, given the appropriate circumstances, will give information on the beneficial ownership of offshore companies and trusts.

Obtaining Residence in the Cayman Islands

Given their low-tax status, the Caymans are often used as a 'pit stop' by wealthy individuals moving to the United States. Typically they stop off in tax havens such as this and transfer assets to offshore companies or trusts before becoming US resident and subject to US taxes on their worldwide income and capital gains.

British, Americans, Canadian and many other Commonwealth citizens do not require a visa to enter, nor do most EU citizens.

If you would like to live on the islands, you have to apply to the Chief Immigration Officer for an initial six-month residence permit. After that you can apply for permanent residence.

As with most of the Caribbean tax havens, if you want to obtain residence you will need to prove that you won't be a drain on the local economy.

This means you must have sufficient income or cash to support yourself and your family and you'll also need to invest *at least* US$180,000 in property or a local business. There is a one-time fee of CI$15,000 on granting of permanent residence (around £11,000).

Permanent residence will allow you live in the islands, provided you do not engage in gainful employment.

Changes to the permanent residence rules were made in 2012. In particular, individuals of "independent means" will now be allowed to remain in the Cayman Islands for the rest of their lives, provided they meet the investment and earnings requirements. Previous residency certificates for those with independent means expired after 25 years.

To be granted the certificate you require an annual income of at least CI$150,000 and must also have invested at least CI$750,000 in the Cayman Islands, of which CI$250,000 or more must be in a property. You also have to prove that you do not have a criminal record and are in good health.

Quality of Life

The beaches are magnificent and if you do move there you can enjoy an excellent standard of living. In fact, Cayman Islands residents have the highest standard of living in the Caribbean.

The cost of living is high (roughly 20% higher than the US) but certainly less than Bermuda and, as always, much will depend on the type of lifestyle you lead.

Note, if you work there you can expect higher wages than in other Caribbean destinations (such as the BVI) to take account of the higher cost of living.

The Caymans are known to be extremely safe and whilst there is petty crime, more serious crime is quite rare.

The property market has experienced a downturn in recent years, so there are bargains to be had. I've seen one four-bedroom beachfront cottage going for $550,000 and another for $290,000, which for the Caymans is dirt cheap! For some of the better beachfront properties you're looking at paying from $2 million to $3 million, up to $6 million but you may be able to beat down the asking prices.

You will find lots of Cayman properties for sale on websites like www.remax.ky and century21cayman.com.

THE CHANNEL ISLANDS

Jersey

Jersey is a self-governing British Crown dependency off the coast of Normandy.

There is no capital gains tax, inheritance tax or wealth tax. There is also a Goods and Services Tax (GST) which increased to 5% from June 2011.

The main tax that residents have to pay is income tax, which is set at a flat rate of 20%.

So although income tax rates are lower than in the UK (where the top tax rate is currently 45%) there are other tax havens with no income tax that may be more attractive.

There was a proposal in Jersey to increase income tax for high earners but this was rejected in April 2011 by Jersey's legislative assembly.

High Net Worth Individuals – 1(1)(k) Status

Jersey is known as one of the most difficult tax havens in which to acquire residence status.

Applications on economic grounds are at the discretion of the Housing Minister, who will take into account factors such as your likely contribution to tax revenues.

To succeed with your application for 1(1)(k) status you will have to be able to provide the Comptroller of Income Tax evidence that you can pay a minimum annual income tax bill of £125,000.

There are currently approximately 130 individuals with 1(1)(k) status and they contribute £13.5 million in tax per year.

If your application is successful, you can only buy an 'approved' property. These typically cost £1 million or more.

The first £625,000 of a qualified person's income is taxed at 20%. This leads to a minimum tax contribution of £125,000. Any income above £625,000 is taxed at a rate of 1%.

Many structure their investments prior to moving to the island to ensure that their assets are outside Jersey and that they only pay the minimum tax.

Essential Employees – 1(1)(j) Status

It may be easier to obtain residence in Jersey by getting a job there (but it's by no means guaranteed). This is known as 'J Category' residence and is usually not permanent – three to five years is typical.

The island's Housing Committee will typically only let you in if no suitably qualified local can be found to do the job – which shouldn't be too difficult if you have specialist skills.

Offshore Companies and Trusts

Even if you cannot acquire 1(1)(k) or 1(1)(j) status there's nothing to stop you from setting up an offshore trust or company in Jersey.

Most Jersey companies are subject to 0% corporate income tax. Financial services companies pay 10%. There were certain deemed distribution provisions, however these have been repealed from January 2012.

Jersey is also a well-known trust jurisdiction. The main benefit is that when the beneficiaries of a trust are non-resident, there is no local tax charged on foreign income and local bank interest. This makes Jersey trusts popular with UK residents.

The lack of double tax treaties reduces the attractiveness of the island as a holding company destination. However, if you're looking to avoid capital gains tax or just reduce income tax, it could be a good choice.

Jersey has agreed to implement the OECD Exchange of Information treaty and has signed an agreement with the UK.

This allows HM Revenue & Customs (HMRC) to ask for the bank account details of any company that could be liable for income tax, corporation tax, capital gains tax or VAT in the UK.

Buying Property in Jersey

Property prices are quite steep compared with many regions of the UK but more reasonable than some parts of the South East. There are also restrictions on property ownership by foreigners.
For property listings go to:

www.ecpw.co.uk

Guernsey

There is no capital gains tax, inheritance tax, or wealth tax.

There is also no VAT or sales tax.

The main tax is income tax, levied at 20%. Allowable deductions include pension contributions and interest on your main residence (within certain limits).

Those who are resident but not principally resident in Guernsey, who go there for employment purposes, can be taxed on their Guernsey earnings and only any other income remitted to Guernsey.

Those who are resident but not principally resident and cannot benefit from the above migrant worker's regime can elect to pay tax on their worldwide income or can pay an annual standard charge of £27,500 plus tax on Guernsey source income (but not bank interest). The standard charge can be offset against tax payable on Guernsey income.

Those who are solely or principally resident in Guernsey are taxed on their worldwide income but may be able to benefit from a £110,000 tax cap (non-Guernsey source income only) or £220,000 tax cap (Guernsey and non-Guernsey source income).

Companies are taxed at 0%. Banking operations are taxed at 10% and property rental and development activities at 20%. This system is under review by the States of Guernsey Policy Council on the basis that it is not within the EU Code of Conduct. However, it will probably only be changed if doing so does not place Guernsey at a competitive disadvantage.

Alderney & Sark

If you're looking for cheaper property prices and a more sedate way of life, the Channel Island of Alderney may be worth considering. It offers the same tax advantages as Jersey and Guernsey but is much smaller. Alderney companies will also benefit from the new 0/10 regime (0% tax for most companies; 10% for some financial companies).

Even quieter still is Sark. This is classed as part of the Bailiwick of Guernsey but has no income tax laws. The only real tax there is a form of wealth tax, on the value of a resident's assets (but even this is limited to £3,500!).

THE COOK ISLANDS

This is one of the less-known tax havens. The Cook Islands are extremely isolated geographically, located half way between New Zealand and Hawaii. The population is a mere 21,000!

There is no capital gains tax, inheritance tax or wealth tax. However, it's not a nil-tax haven. Income tax is payable by those residing and working on the islands and is levied on a sliding scale with rates of 25% and 30%.
In terms of companies, a resident company would be subject to tax of 20% on its worldwide profits.

There is VAT of 12.5% and there is also stamp duty. The Cook Islands have no double tax treaties.

Doesn't sound too good? Well I'd agree, except for the fact that offshore companies and trusts do not pay any taxes except for stamp duty.

There are about 15,000 offshore entities and the sector has been growing quite rapidly in recent years. Confidentiality is tight, except in cases of criminal activity, which does not include tax crime.

The Cook Islands have agreed to implement the OECD Exchange of Information Treaty and is on the OECD white list.

All in all, the Cook Islands are a useful place to base an offshore company but most people would not want to become resident there. Not only are they in the middle of nowhere, personal tax rates (except capital gains tax) are quite high.

If you did want to live there, you would have to drastically change your way of life. As you would expect it's a very simple lifestyle revolving around the beach and most people are incredibly laid back.

You won't be eating your usual produce and would need to adapt to the local diet, although other products can be imported from New Zealand. There are hardly any cash machines on the island, although there are a couple of banks. There are some fine restaurants, particularly on the main island (Rarotonga). As you would expect, crime is very low and the weather is warm pretty much all year round (with a rainy season from November to March).

All land in the Cook Islands is leasehold (up to 60 years). To be allowed to buy a lease you have to be either a Cook Islander or permanent resident, start a business or buy an existing business.

The Entry Residence and Departure Act demands that anyone other than Cook Islanders and permanent residents who wish to live and work in the islands must first obtain a work and residence permit.

If you wish to become a permanent resident you need to either marry a local, gain local employment and live there for five years, or invest in a local company or business (the amounts vary from NZ$500,000 to NZ$1 million).

Generally speaking, it's difficult to get permanent residence in the Cook Islands, particularly compared with other jurisdictions that offer much easier residency requirements.

COSTA RICA

Costa Rica is a Central American tax haven, located between Panama and Nicaragua. In tax terms, Costa Rica is highly attractive as it taxes on the basis of *territoriality*.

Remember Barbados, which only taxes overseas income of non-domiciliaries if the cash is brought into the country? Well the territoriality principle takes this one step further and simply doesn't tax overseas income. This principle of territoriality is the key aspect of the Costa Rican tax regime and only income earned within Costa Rica is subject to tax.

So, provided a resident keeps his income-producing assets outside Costa Rica, there is no tax payable. Remember, however, that any locally earned income, for example from a trade carried on from Costa Rica, could be subject to local taxes at rates of up to 25%. However, if you're employed in Costa Rica the maximum tax rate is 15%.

There is also no capital gains tax in Costa Rica, aside from a limited tax that applies to certain gains derived from the normal trade of business of the seller. This tax is levied at a maximum rate of 30%. If you dispose of property or shares, this tax will mostly not apply.

In terms of lifestyle, Costa Rica is probably the most expensive country in Central America but that doesn't mean you can't live there cheaply.

The sales tax of 13% bumps up the cost of goods but utility bills and the cost of local products are cheap – it tends to be only imported goods that are expensive.

Communications are very good with an excellent telephone system and internet access and the climate is mild most of the year.

Central America has a poor reputation in terms of crime and personal security and although Costa Rica is probably the safest, you would still need to be vigilant.

Property prices are very low and Costa Rica has been touted as one of the next property investment hot spots.

Unfortunately it's difficult to arrange finance if you're a foreigner and you'd need to arrange this in another country or become a resident.

Property is a fair bit cheaper than some of the other more cosmopolitan tax havens but prices are a lot higher than when we first started publishing this guide.

A two-bedroom beach condo can be picked up for between $150,000 and $200,000 and I've seen one beautiful villa with ocean views going for around $400,000 and another three-bedroom house, without views, going for around $288,000.

Cheaper property can be found in the Central Valley region, where homes are available for 50% less than those on the Pacific coast.

Becoming Resident in Costa Rica

The authorities offer a number of residence programmes that make it relatively easy to establish yourself as a Costa-Rican resident.

One of the best schemes is the 'rentista' scheme, which applies to foreigners with guaranteed income.

In order to obtain residence under this scheme you need to show that you have a guaranteed income of at least $2,500 per month for at least two years.

The most common way to prove this is by means of a notarized letter from a bank, confirming that you have at least $150,000 on deposit. You do not have to keep the money in a Costa Rican bank.

You must agree to transfer at least $2,500 per month to Costa Rica and live in the country for at least four months per year.

You (and your dependent family) will then be entitled to live in Costa Rica for five years and take advantage of the tax exemption for non-Costa Rican income.

It is also possible to qualify under the 'pensionado' programme. You must have at least $1,000 per month from a pension scheme, change at least this amount per month from dollars into colons (the local currency) and live in Costa Rica for at least four months per year.

Both rentistas and pensionados can set up their own businesses but cannot work for someone else without a work permit.

Corporation Tax

Domestic companies face a high tax bill, with a top corporation tax rate of 30% (a 10% rate applies to small companies that earn less than $91,000), and there is also a social security tax of 26.17% of gross wages.

However, Costa Rican companies are still popular as the territoriality principle applies to companies as well as individuals. Therefore, offshore companies carrying out no activities in Costa Rica, or holding no Costa Rican assets, can avoid local taxes altogether.

In addition, the country has no double tax treaties but does have a longstanding exchange of information treaty with the US.

Although Costa Rica was on the OECD blacklist for not agreeing to implement the OECD Exchange of Information Treaty, it has subsequently agreed to implement the provisions. It has now signed in excess of 12 agreements and is on the OECD whitelist.

All in all, Costa Rica offers good opportunities for individuals looking to shelter offshore income and gains and allows you to establish yourself offshore at a reasonable price.

CYPRUS

Cyprus is one of Europe's key tax havens and is only a four-hour flight from the UK. It's a popular destination for those wanting to avoid capital gains tax and is becoming increasingly popular as a home for setting up offshore structures.

One of the key benefits of Cyprus is that it has double-tax treaties with well over 45 other countries, including most major Western 'high-tax' countries and most Central and Eastern European states. This is unusual for a tax haven and means that Cyprus is a very good choice for holding companies and investment companies.

Cyprus is also on the OECD 'white list' and has implemented numerous tax information exchange agreements.

Income tax rates vary from 20% to 35% but there is a generous €19,500 exemption (similar to the UK personal allowance).

Retiring to Cyprus

Those who receive a pension from outside Cyprus enjoy a special 5% tax rate, with an annual exemption of €3,420.

The low tax rate is extremely attractive for UK retirees because the double tax agreement between the UK and Cyprus allows UK pensions to be paid without any UK income tax deducted.

In other words, most pensioners living in the UK will face a marginal income tax rate of either 20% or 40%. Those who move to Cyprus will pay just 5%.

There are lots of other tax exemptions in Cyprus. All of the following are free of income tax:

- Interest received by individuals
- 50% of interest income of companies
- Dividends
- Profits of permanent establishments carrying on a trade abroad
- Profits from the sale of shares

- Income from employment services provided abroad to a non-resident employer

However, Cyprus does levy a 'special contribution for defence' on certain types of income for residents. Interest income is now subject to a 15% charge, whereas dividends are subject to a 20% charge from 2012.

Cyprus also offers an attractive capital gains tax (CGT) regime. CGT is levied at the rate of 20% on gains arising from the disposal of land and property *situated in Cyprus* or the disposal of shares in a company (excluding shares of listed companies) which owns land or property situated in Cyprus.

There is also an exemption from CGT on the transfer of such assets between close family members (e.g. between spouses or children).

If a resident of Cyprus owns property overseas there is no CGT payable in Cyprus when the property is sold. So a disposal of UK property would not be subject to tax in Cyprus if you are a Cyprus resident.

Cyprus has gained increased prominence due to its treaties with Eastern European countries. These enable a Cyprus legal entity to extract profits from Eastern European countries at a reduced tax rate or with no tax payable at all. This is thanks to the nil (or low) rates of withholding taxes on dividends, interest and royalties laid out in the treaties.

Given that many Eastern European countries are seeing increased inward investment, the interest in Cyprus companies (in order to take advantage of these low withholding taxes) is likely to continue growing.

The treaty with Russia, for example, allows a Cyprus holding company to incur withholding tax at 5% on dividends and royalties from a Russian subsidiary, rather than the standard 15%. In addition, the Cyprus company will be exempt from income tax on the dividend income and may be able to claim an exemption from the 20% defence fund contribution.

Company Taxation

Cyprus now has a 12.5% corporate tax rate, which applies to all companies. This gives Cyprus one of the lowest corporation tax rates in Europe.

Unlike the UK and the US, the shareholders are not liable to income tax on dividends when profits are extracted from a company, although any resident shareholders must pay the 15% special contribution to defence (if you are non-resident you are exempt from this payment).

Dividends received from a company located in Cyprus or abroad are generally exempt from corporation tax.

Tax Sparing Provisions

It's also worth noting that a number of the tax treaties Cyprus has entered into have tax-sparing provisions. A tax-sparing provision means that, even if income is tax free in Cyprus, it can still be given as a tax credit in the other country, as if tax had already been paid (in other words, you get a tax credit even though you haven't paid any tax).

These tax-sparing provisions are usually given by developed countries to developing countries to encourage investment and economic development.

The taxes all or partly spared include:

• Tax on interest paid on economic development loans (Canada, Denmark, Germany, France, UK).
• Tax relieved because of deductions related to investment in Cyprus (Canada, UK).

Living in Cyprus

Cyprus is a good choice for Europeans as it's not too far from home but offers an excellent low-tax environment with a low cost of living. In fact it's one of the cheapest countries in Europe and this is a big advantage for potential immigrants, particularly pensioners.

It's a totally different environment when compared with some of the Caribbean tax havens, many of which are, by and large, developing countries, albeit with some highly developed areas.

Cyprus is a well developed country with excellent communication and transport links and a good choice of restaurants, department stores and everything else to make it a home from home. (In other words, you won't have to go without your favourite snacks and other home comforts!).

Weather wise, it's a Mediterranean island with a lot of sunshine! From March to November you will probably enjoy glorious weather. The rest of the year will be cooler and there will probably be rain in January and February – although after experiencing 40 degrees every day you will probably be glad of the change.

Cyprus is also a good choice for parents with young children as the schools are generally good and you can choose between state and private schools.

The crime rate is very low compared with other western European states but it has been increasing.

It's also easier for European residents to establish residence in Cyprus now that it's part of the EU. In order to be classed as a Cypriot resident you need to spend at least 183 days in the country during the tax year.

Cyprus Property

Once a favourite choice amongst UK property investors, the Cyprus property market has crashed in recent years.

In 2010 the Cyprus housing market was the third worst performer in the EU according to the Knight Frank Global House Price Index, with prices slumping by 9% (the worst, not surprisingly, was Ireland with a fall of 11%, followed by Lithuania with a 10% fall).

Properties in areas that were popular with investors experienced the worst falls. Prices in Paralimni/Famagusta plummeted by 23%.

To make matters worse, many investors took out Swiss Franc mortgages that were hit hard by the strength of the Swiss Franc relative to the pound and Euro, resulting in many British expats being unable to afford their mortgage repayments.

For example, back in 2007 a CHF 250,000 mortgage would cost around £100,000 to repay. Now it will cost around £170,000 to pay off.

Developers have been offering 'discounts' of 30% or more as well as other incentives but have still struggled to shift property.

For those with their hearts set on a property in Cyprus, prices start at around €40,000 for one-bedroom apartments. Three-bedroom detached family homes are listed from €200,000. (See Cyprusprop.com for lots more listings).

A lot of properties have had their prices reduced and one can only assume that most of the asking prices are wishful thinking.

All in all, you can safely assume that Cyprus is a buyer's market and, if you want to buy a property, you should drive an extremely hard bargain and be very careful (buying any asset in a declining market can be like catching a falling knife).

In summary, Cyprus is one of the top tax havens for UK pensioners and anyone wanting to wipe out a big capital gains tax bill. Its popularity has increased due to the lifestyle, low cost of living and booming property prices. Cypriot offshore companies are also popular, particularly for investment in Eastern Europe and holding companies.

DUBAI

Dubai has become an increasingly popular destination for UK expats who want to earn a tax-free salary.

Dubai is a nil-tax haven for individuals. There is no:

- Personal income tax
- Capital gains tax
- Inheritance tax
- Sales tax

Dubai, therefore, holds up well against the other tax haven states. As a bonus it also has about 45 tax treaties (because it is part of the United Arab Emirates), which is rare for a tax haven, although these tend to mainly benefit Dubai companies, allowing reduced withholding taxes on dividends and restricting tax overseas.

Dubai is also on the OECD 'white list' for having a number of Exchange of Information treaties.

Setting Up an Offshore Company in Dubai

As well as the personal tax benefits, Dubai is becoming of more importance as a home for offshore companies.

It's certainly not cheap to set up a company there (you are looking at about $5,000 to incorporate and annual renewal fees are in the region of $2,500) but the benefit, of course, is the zero tax rates.

Note, when forming a company, you would probably be looking at setting one up in one of the special zones available to expats. The Jebel Ali free zone is the most popular.

If privacy and confidentiality is important to you, you may need to consider the impact of any double tax treaty. These will often contain exchange of information provisions and can be used by overseas tax authorities to request information from the Dubai tax authorities (for example, details of second homes owned in Dubai).

A common technique, particularly for e-commerce businesses, is to form an offshore company such as a Panama or British Virgin Islands IBC and to register it in one of the free trade zones. The Dubai Internet City (DIC) is a free trade zone specifically for e-commerce businesses.

Free trade zones offer renewable 50-year tax holidays and exemption from import duty on goods brought into the free zone.

The combination of Dubai and a good offshore jurisdiction such as the British Virgin Islands would ensure that there would be no disclosure of shareholders and only limited disclosure of the directors (potentially only nominee directors), so reinforcing the asset protection benefits.

Buying Property in Dubai

Dubai's property market suffered more than most during the global economic downturn with prices falling by between 50% and 70%.

There are reports that the market has been recovering thanks to cheaper mortgage interest rates (under 5%) and the scrapping of some mortgage arrangement fees.

Apparently prices in luxury developments such as Arabian Ranches and Palm Jumeirah are no longer being adjusted downwards, which suggests that the market could, at the very least, be close to the bottom.

You should bear in mind that you will not have free rein to buy property wherever you choose in Dubai. Non-residents can only buy property inside special zones and are mainly restricted to new developments.

Currently, one-bedroom apartments start at around £100,000, rising to over £1 million at the Palm Jebel Ali Water Homes.

If it's space for a family you are after, three-bedroom houses are available from around £285,000 and some lovely homes are available for around £400,000.

Of course, this being Dubai, there are also high-end luxury homes available with multimillion dollar price tags to match.

A concern of more cautious property investors is how the local succession laws will apply to their property if they die. This is a complex area but there are specific forced succession rules that are likely to be different to those in most European countries.

For this reason, a lot of expats opt to own Dubai property via an offshore company. The benefit of this is that the shares in the company can usually be transferred in accordance with your home country's rules of succession.

Living in Dubai

Unless you're a visitor from certain Arab states, you will need to obtain a visa. For example, if you are going there on holiday, the tour operator will usually get you a 14-day or 30-day tourist visa.

If you buy a freehold property costing at least one million UAE dirham (approximately £167,000) and have monthly income of at least 10,000 dirham (£1,668) you are entitled to apply for a six-month visa that can be renewed at the airport. It is difficult to ascertain just how valuable this visa is. Our feeling is that it is too short to be of practical use.

In terms of lifestyle, Dubai is known to be an excellent place to live, with a very low crime rate and very good schools and medical facilities, although you will probably need to pay for a private international school for your children.

Dubai is well known for its shopping facilities and, apart from over 50 large shopping centres, there are also the local markets, or souks, where you can pick up bargains (if you're prepared to haggle!).

Hi-tech goods such as computers and other home electronic devices can be bought at bargain prices. The overall cost of living is also very reasonable (you can buy a kebab for just 50p).

Remember that Dubai is a Muslim country and, as such, you will need to respect the rules. Having said that, it's fair to say that Dubai is probably the most Western of the United Arab Emirates (as you would expect with over 50% of the population being expats) and therefore the rules are not as strict as in other Muslim countries.

As a result, you can still obtain alcohol in restaurants and hotels and, although Arabic is the official language, most people speak English.

Overall, Dubai is a good tax haven option. The downside, of course, is that it's located in a politically sensitive area of the world. While the United Arab Emirates has not been the subject of any significant religious or political tension, this is not to say that this state of affairs will not change in the future.

EASTERN EUROPE

Maybe not your first choice of tax havens, the countries of Eastern Europe are certainly worth knowing about given the rapid economic growth being enjoyed and the flood of investors looking for bargain properties in recent years.

Many of the Eastern European states levy flat taxes. This is perhaps the most simple of all taxes as everyone's income is taxed at the same rate. The thinking is that, if the rate is set low enough, most people won't mind coughing up and the black economy will shrink – resulting in greater tax collections than before.

Having said this, there are only a couple of Eastern European states that offer tax rates as low as many of the tax havens you'll read about in this book. Below are the income tax rates in some of the Eastern European countries:

- Estonia   21%
- Latvia   24%
- Lithuania   15%
- Serbia   10%
- Ukraine   15%
- Bulgaria   10%
- Slovakia   19%
- Romania   16%
- Hungary   16%
- Russia   13%

There are also Eastern European countries that levy tax on a normal 'progressive basis'. (In other words, the more you earn, the higher the tax rate.) For example, Croatia can tax at rates of up to 40%.

Looking at the above list, the only really low-tax states are Russia, Bulgaria and Serbia.

In terms of capital gains, most of these states class gains as additional income, however there are some specific rules, particularly in relation to land and property disposals, that are worth remembering. These could be of use to budding overseas property investors who want to make profits in emerging markets.

Croatia has high rates of income tax and taxes gains on land at a standard rate of 25%. There is a tax exemption if the property is your main residence or if you've owned it for at least three years.

Russia classes gains as additional income (which would be subject to the 13% income tax rate for residents) but will exempt gains completely if you've owned the property for at least three years.

Slovakia exempts property gains if the property is either your main residence (for at least two years) or if you've owned the property for at least five years. Lithuania exempts Lithuanian property if you've owned it for at least three years.

Russia and most East European countries also do not have any inheritance tax. Therefore, on the plus side, Russia looks good in terms of both low overall tax rates and the potential exemption for property gains. As with most of the Eastern European states, Russia adopts the usual method of determining your residence status. Anyone actually in Russia for more than 183 days in the calendar year is considered a resident for tax purposes. You would then need to file a Russian personal income tax return.

Entry to and from Russia is tightly controlled and you would need to get yourself a visa from a Russian Embassy. There are different types: tourist, business, etc and each has different qualifying conditions and allows you to spend a specified period in Russia.

It used to be difficult to obtain a visa. However, with new visa provisions introduced in 2007, it's now much simpler and a number of online companies will arrange one for you. The business visa is generally preferred as this allows you to spend up to 12 months in the country. In order to live there on even a semi-permanent basis you would need to get a residence permit. These are difficult to obtain, unless you were born in Russia or are married to a Russian citizen. The first step would be to get a temporary visa, which could then be upgraded to a permanent visa.

In terms of exchange of information the Russian Federation is on the OECD 'white list' and is party to numerous exchange of information treaties.

All in all, if you want to access a developing economy, Russia may be an option and the low taxes would be an added bonus.

GIBRALTAR

Gibraltar is one of the well-established European tax havens. It's a self governing but dependent territory of the United Kingdom.

Gibraltar is popular with wealthy UK expats because it is so British and relatively easy to move to.

It has a nice Mediterranean climate and the crime rate is very low. On the downside it is very densely populated (less than six square kilometres in area but a population of over 30,000 Gibraltarians).

Gibraltar is a 'low-tax' haven rather than a 'no-tax' haven.

There is no capital gains tax, inheritance tax or VAT but, as you've probably guessed, there is income tax… and it can be quite high, with a top rate of 40%.

You will be resident in Gibraltar if you spend at least 183 days there in any 12-month period. You will then be subject to Gibraltar tax on your worldwide income.

However, if you are moving to Gibraltar to exploit the tax-saving opportunities you should be looking at obtaining High Net Worth Individual status (HNWI) – pronounced hun-wee.

HNWIs are also known as Category 2 status individuals.

HNWIs are allowed to live in Gibraltar with their spouses and children and enjoy a special tax regime. HNWIs are liable to pay a minimum income tax charge of £22,000 even if they have no income arising in Gibraltar or remitted to Gibraltar.

If income is remitted to Gibraltar or arises in Gibraltar only the first £80,000 is taxable resulting in a maximum tax charge of £29,080 for the current 2014 tax year.

To keep your tax bill closer to £22,000 than £29,080, you would have to remit as little income as possible to Gibraltar.

HNWI status will mostly appeal to those with very high taxable incomes. Clearly, you would have to be paying more than £22,000 or £29,080 in UK income tax to make it worthwhile from a tax-saving perspective (i.e. this means you would have to be earning more than approximately £80,000 or £100,000 per year).

It's also worth noting, however, that your spouse's income can be included with your income. In other words, there will only be one maximum tax charge of £29,080 per family.

Furthermore, HNWIs enjoy other tax benefits including:

- No inheritance tax
- No capital gains tax
- No tax on interest earned in foreign bank accounts
- No tax on dividend payments
- No tax on occupational pension payments

How to Become a HNWI

In order to qualify the following conditions must be satisfied:

- You must have a net worth of at least £2 million.
- You must own or rent accommodation that is approved by the Gibraltar Finance Centre. The property must be used by you and your direct family (ie not rented out).
- You must not have been Gibraltar resident during the preceding five years. You would be resident if you spent 183 days or more in any tax year or an average of 90 days in any three of the previous five years.
- You cannot run a business or get a job in Gibraltar. There are, however, exceptions to this rule, e.g. if you are a director of a Gibraltar Exempt Company or a director of a company that does not conduct any business in Gibraltar.
- You must have private medical cover in Gibraltar.

There is no minimum period you must stay in Gibraltar, as long as all of the above conditions are satisfied. Your residency certificate will have to be endorsed every three years.

Applications are sent to the Finance Centre and must include two references (one from a bank confirming your financial standing), a detailed

CV, evidence of ownership or rental of a property and a certified copy of your passport.

There is a non-refundable application fee of £1,000.

Company Tax

As for companies, the rate of tax for companies was reduced from 22% to 10% with effect from 1 January 2011.

Capital gains are tax free, as are dividends, interest income and royalties. Gibraltar has no double tax treaties but relief is available for tax paid in other countries.

Gibraltar also has an attractive trust regime. Trusts created by non-residents that generate overseas income are exempt from Gibraltar income tax.

In terms of the exchange of information provisions, Gibraltar has implemented the OECD Exchange of Information Treaty and is on the OECD white list.

Buying Property in Gibraltar

High-quality property is notoriously expensive and has risen a lot since we first started publishing this guide. This is due to a combination of high demand and limited supply due to the shortage of space.

In addition, if you're looking for a luxury villa with grounds, you're likely to be disappointed, as most developments are apartments.

Having said that, the property market has slowed down and there is a broad spread of property available.

In between that you can pick up three-bedroom apartments for as little as £370,000 and many have stunning views over the Bay of Gibraltar. A three-bedroom duplex with a swimming pool in the popular South District will set you back between £900,000 and £1 million.

If you decide to rent instead of buying, you can rent two bedrooms for between £1,500 and £2,500 per month and three bedrooms for between £2,000 and £3,000 per month.

For more listings go to: www.bfagib.com

On the plus side, if you're a British citizen you are allowed to live and work in Gibraltar without obtaining a residence permit. If you aren't British but are from an EU country, you will need to get a residence permit (and show sufficient income to support yourself). If you are not from the EU it is much more difficult as you'll need to get a work permit first before applying for a residence permit.

Gibraltar has a lot to offer on many different fronts: low taxes (especially if you obtain HNWI status), a beautiful climate, close proximity to most European countries, British culture and reasonable property prices compared with some of the more exclusive tax havens.

HONG KONG

Hong Kong is one of the most famous tax havens in the world. It's not a nil-tax haven but has a very simple system that allows many expats to complete their tax returns in minutes.
Hong Kong has the following tax rates:

- 16.5% for companies
- 15% for unincorporated businesses
- 2%-17% for salaries and pensions

There is no capital gains tax or inheritance tax in Hong Kong.

There are also personal allowances that can be deducted from salaries – HK$120,000 for single taxpayers (£10,100) and HK$240,000 for married couples (£20,200).

These personal allowances are increased significantly if you have children.

Deductions are also available for certain education expenses, home loan interest and contributions to retirement schemes.

The personal income tax rate is capped at the standard rate of 15% (no personal allowances allowed).

Territorial Tax System

The beauty of the Hong Kong tax regime is that it also applies the territorial basis of tax. So only profits and income actually earned within Hong Kong are taxed.

This means that overseas investment income and overseas salaries can be completely exempt from local income tax. Hong Kong also offers an advance clearance procedure, which lets you find out for certain whether or not the authorities will tax your income.

Most expats living in Hong Kong will therefore be taxed only on local salary income or local trading profits.

Most Hong Kong residents pay no tax at all (thanks to high personal allowances), however expats with high salaries will be subject to the flat rate of 15%. Additionally, if you're in Hong Kong for not more than 60 days per tax year, you are not liable for Hong Kong tax.

Hong Kong is a sound location for offshore company incorporation with some cheap incorporation packages available for up to HK$10,000 (around $1,300). The only downside here is the lack of double tax treaties.

Hong Kong has however agreed to work with the OECD to sign tax information exchange agreements with various developed economies.
Residency Requirements

The downside to using Hong Kong as a tax haven is the strict entrance requirements.

Unless you are going there under a contract of employment (in which case you will obtain an Employment Visa), your best bet may be either the Investment Visa or the Capital Investment Entrant Visa.

The business investor scheme is for individuals wanting to establish a business in Hong Kong that will boost the economy and employ locals.
The preferred option is likely to be the Capital Investment Entrant Visa which allows you to obtain residence by making an investment in certain permissible investments.

Prior to 14 October 2010 you were able to qualify if you had HK$6.5 million (around £550,000) in 'permissible investment assets'. You also have to show that you can support yourself.

However, from 14 October 2010, the qualifying investment threshold has been increased to HK$10 million (around £840,000).

Real estate is not included on the list of permissible investment assets. However, the following are all permissible investments:

- Shares in companies quoted on the Hong Kong Stock Exchange.
- Certain bonds, denominated in HK$.
- Certain certificates of deposit, denominated in HK$.
- Certain subordinated debt
- Eligible funds that invest in Hong Kong and Chinese companies.

More information:

http://www.immd.gov.hk/en/services/hk-visas/capital-investment-entrant.html

Hong Kong Property

Hong Kong housing prices rose by 11% in 2011 but the rate of growth has since slown in response to various cooling measures introduced by the Government and as the banks gradually increase mortgage rates.

You can find Hong Kong properties to rent or buy on these websites:

- http://residential.savillsproperty.com/main/Home.aspx
- www.hongkonghomes.com
- www.squarefoot.com.hk

IRELAND

Ireland has traditionally been a popular retirement destination and a bolthole for writers and artists lured by the artists' tax exemption. However, since 2007 this income tax exemption has been reduced and in Finance Act 2011 a cap of €40,000 was introduced.

Ireland is certainly not one of the nil-tax havens and would fall firmly in the low-tax category. The Irish levy income tax and capital gains tax (33%) and there is also inheritance tax.

Income Tax

For single taxpayers, income tax is levied at 20% on the first €32,800 and 41% on the balance.

For married couples, income tax is levied on each spouse at 20% on the first €41,800 and 41% on the balance.

Personal tax credits that can be deducted from the tax due: €1,650 for single taxpayers and €3,300 for married couples.

There is also a universal social charge: 2% for annual income up to €10,036, 4% for income between €10,037 and €16,016 and 7% for income above €16,016. This will be capped at 4% for anyone with a medical card.

Non-Domiciled Individuals

The tax rates in Ireland are quite high but there are tax benefits for individuals who are non-domiciled.

In effect, a 'foreign' person resident in Ireland has only needed to pay tax on income brought into Ireland (the so-called remittance basis), so most income could be kept offshore to avoid paying any income tax.

In fact, if a suitable distinction is made between capital and subsequent income from capital before you take up permanent residence (for example, using capital and income accounts – see Chapter 11) it may even be possible to live in Ireland almost completely tax free.

This favourable tax treatment used to be available to Irish citizens who are non-ordinarily resident (non-resident for at least three consecutive years) but this concession was abolished in the 2010 Finance Act.

Irish citizens who return to Ireland after a long period abroad have to pay tax on their worldwide income when they commence Irish residence.

From 1 January 2010, the remittance basis of tax is only available to individuals who are not domiciled in Ireland.

Irish Resident Status

Your residence status for Irish tax purposes is determined by the number of days you spend in the country during the tax year.

You will be classed as Irish resident if:

- You spend 183 days or more in the country during the tax year, or
- You spend 280 days or more in Ireland over a period of two consecutive tax years. You will then be regarded as resident in Ireland for the second tax year.

(However, if you spend 30 days or less in the country in either tax year, those days will not be taken into account when calculating if you have breached the 280-day limit.)

High Net Worth Individuals

The 2010 Finance Act introduced a Domicile Levy of €200,000 on wealthy individuals who are Irish domiciled, regardless of where they live, and who have:

- An Irish income tax liability of less than €200,000 and
- Worldwide income of more than €1 million, and
- Irish situated capital valued at €5 million or more

This looks to be similar to the US tax basis of taxing US citizens on worldwide income, irrespective of their residence.

Corporation Tax

The Irish corporate tax regime is one of the most attractive in the world thanks to a combination of low tax rates and lots of tax treaties that Irish resident companies can take advantage of.

Irish companies are taxed on trading income at a rate of just 12.5%. This only applies to trading income and the rate applied to non-trading income is 25%.

This is one of the lowest rates of corporation tax in Europe, just behind the Isle of Man and the Channel Islands, which currently have a 0% rate, and some Eastern European countries which have a 10% corporation tax rate. It is one of the lowest in any developed economy in the world. So it's not surprising that Ireland's offshore sector has boomed.

As you'd expect, Ireland is on the OECD 'white list' and has numerous exchange of information agreements for tax purposes.

Ireland has been a very popular alternative 'offshore' choice for many multinationals, which have transferred some of their operations to Irish companies to reduce their overall effective tax rates.

Ireland therefore offers tax-saving opportunities at both the corporate and personal level.

Living in Ireland

As for actually living and working there, EU nationals don't need a residence or work permit but residents of most non-EU countries (except for the US, Australia and Canada) will need a residence and work permit.

Another reason why Ireland has been a popular choice with EU expats is that there are no restrictions on the purchase of property (unlike many of the other tax havens).

The climate is mild, the country has excellent transport and communication links and the level of crime, particularly violent crime, is low.

The bad news, of course, is that the Irish economy is a disaster zone: GDP has fallen by 7% over the last 12 months alone and the unemployment rate is 15%.

Fifteen years ago, Irish citizens working in the UK and other countries started returning home to take advantage of the booming economy. Now they're leaving in droves (over 100,000 Irish are expected to have emigrated in 2012 and 2013).

This only matters if you are looking for a job there or want to start a business selling to locals.
For certain other people there probably hasn't been a better time to move to Ireland since the 1980s. Why? Because house prices have crashed. This is bad news for local homeowners but great news for anyone wanting to go and live in the country and buy a property.

Irish Property

Property prices have always been reasonable in many parts of the country but were astronomical in Dublin a few years ago, fuelled by low Eurozone interest rates.

However, the country's property market went into freefall in 2009. Prices in Dublin have fallen by an estimated 50% from their peak (there are no published land registry figures).

You can find properties to rent or buy on these websites:

- **www.myhome.ie**
- **www.daft.ie**
- **www.property.ie**

THE ISLE OF MAN

The Isle of Man (IOM) is located just off the west coast of England, approximately 70 miles from Liverpool. In comparison with other tax havens it definitely falls into the 'low-tax' rather than no-tax category.

There are generous income tax allowances for individuals and married couples. For example, for a married couple, the first £18,600 of income is automatically tax free. The next £21,000 is taxed at 10%, with income above this taxed at just 20%.

To attract more 'high-net-worth individuals and active entrepreneurs' the total tax payable is capped: no resident will pay more than £120,000 in tax.

There is also no capital gains tax (CGT) or inheritance tax.

The island is therefore a good place to live if you want to avoid paying tax when you sell your property portfolio.

In comparison with many of the other tax havens, Manx tax exiles tend to be quite understated. You won't find a harbour full of expensive yachts or Ferraris parked on every street corner. The island is a lot more 'gritty' than some of the other boltholes of the rich and famous.

The IOM nevertheless offers a good quality of life, provided you don't mind the weather. It has good education and health services and a very low crime rate. Violent crime, in particular is low, as is car theft (it's difficult to get cars off an island).

Many potential emigrants would probably look further afield and for some it's difficult to see the attraction of a cold island off the coast of England, especially when there are tax havens offering much warmer climates and equally attractive tax laws. However, the Isle of Man attracts more than its fair share of expats and over 50% of the population weren't actually born there – after all, it's close to the UK, easy to emigrate to and property prices are quite reasonable compared with other European tax havens.

At the top of the pile you'll find one of the Isle of Man's most impressive houses: a large period country residence set in 10 acres with eight bedrooms, going for £5 million. A bit lower down the scale, £1.5 million will buy you a modern four-bedroom detached house in one of the most desirable areas, with landscaped gardens and panoramic coastal and rural views.

For £430,000 you can buy a very pretty three-bedroom detached bungalow near Douglas (the capital) with rural views and a beautiful secluded garden. At the bottom of the ladder you'll find one-bedroom apartments for £80,000 and two-bedroom apartments for £120,000 and three-bedroom semi-detached houses for less than £215,000.

There are always bargains to be had (for example, a couple of years ago I spotted a six-bedroom mid-terrace house in Douglas going for just £230,000).

The Isle of Man is extremely stable politically as you'd expect, given that it is a UK Crown dependency. The island does, however, run its own affairs and make its own laws.

For UK expats, actually moving over there is pretty easy as well. There is unrestricted access for UK citizens and residents in the European Economic Area.

A 0% corporation tax rate for most trading companies (except banks and some property companies) came into force in 2006. This gives the Isle of Man the joint lowest corporate tax rate in Europe. Note that the 0% rate only applies to trading companies. Non-trading companies will be taxed in the main at 10%.

The Isle of Man used to have an "attribution rule", whereby if less than 55% of an Isle of Man company's profits were extracted, Isle of Man residents would have to pay income tax on their share of the "attributed income". However, this tax has been abolished for accounting periods beginning on 6th April 2012.

In terms of exchange of information, the Isle of Man is on the OECD 'white list' and has implemented numerous exchange of information agreements.

The Isle of Man is therefore a good choice for UK nationals wanting to escape high taxation but remain close to home. In addition, it's growing in popularity as a place for e-commerce businesses to relocate to, due to its sound telecoms infrastructure and 100% broadband coverage.

LIECHTENSTEIN

Liechtenstein is a tiny landlocked country, sandwiched between Switzerland and Austria, with only 35,000 inhabitants.

The official language is German, although English and French are also spoken.

Unlike other tax havens, there are no special rules for offshore entities – in Liechtenstein everybody enjoys low taxes!

Note that I use the term 'low taxes'. There are still taxes, the most common one being income tax. There is also a type of wealth tax called the 'net worth tax' and VAT is levied on most goods and services.
Inheritance tax and gift tax were abolished in 2011.

Whether or not you have to pay tax in Liechtenstein depends on your residence status. You will be classed as resident if:

- You have a property there that you keep as a permanent residence, or
- You are living in Liechtenstein and either have a job or business there.

As with most countries, if you are deemed to be resident you are liable to pay tax on your worldwide income.

Income tax in Liechtenstein is payable on income from your job or business but because there is a wealth tax, there is no income tax on investment income (dividends, interest, rental income etc), provided the underlying assets have been subject to the wealth tax.

Any capital gains are also usually taxed as income, except for certain property disposals, which are taxed separately.

Any tax bill would be reduced by a variety of personal allowances and capital gains annual exemptions, which total between 5,000 and 11,000 Swiss Francs (between £2,000 and £5,000).

Unlike many countries that have a system of independent taxation, married couples are taxed jointly in Liechtenstein. The rate of income tax depends on the level of taxable income and also the area in which the taxpayer is resident.

The maximum marginal rate varies between 3.24% and 24% with the higher tax rate payable on taxable income in excess of CHF180,000 (£80,000).

There is also a system of social security contributions and employees pay this at the rate of 4.3% of gross pay (although the self employed are punished and pay a rate of up to 11%).

The net worth tax is applied to your *net* assets (the market value of your total assets minus your liabilities). Assets include land and property, bank accounts, shares, valuables, works of art etc. Liabilities include debts etc.

When calculating the net worth tax charge, the first CHF20,000 of net assets is usually exempt with the balance taxed on a sliding scale, reaching a maximum marginal rate of about 0.9% on taxable net wealth of about CHF350,000 (£150,000).

Company Tax

As from 1 January 2011 there have been some significant changes to the tax regime in Liechtenstein, including the introduction of a flat corporate income tax rate of 12.5%.

There are a variety of offshore entities that are used to take advantage of the low taxes. Liechtenstein is most famous for its 'Anstalt' and 'Stiftung'.

The Anstalt is a unique form of legal structure with no members or shareholders. It is a separate entity with beneficiaries and, provided it operates as an investment entity, its income could be tax free.

The Stiftung is essentially a Liechtenstein foundation (Chapter 5 has more on the use of foundations). The Liechtenstein foundation was one of the first around and although more expensive than those available in other jurisdictions, it is still popular with the very wealthy, thanks to the high level of confidentiality and privacy offered.

Bank Secrecy

Liechtenstein has traditionally had strong bank secrecy and used to consider information exchange only in cases of tax fraud and other criminal activity. It has, however, signed up to the EU Savings Tax Directive and will be applying a withholding tax rather than sharing information (for more about this directive see Chapter 9).

The strong privacy benefits of Liechtenstein have been diminished by heavy pressure from the international community. In early 2008, Germany (and then the UK) obtained information that a number of wealthy residents were using Liechtenstein foundations to avoid tax.

Following this, Liechtenstein has agreed to implement exchange of information agreements with various other countries and has signed up to the OECD Exchange of Information Treaty. At the date of publication, Liechtenstein is on the OECD white list and has negotiated more than 12 exchange of information treaties.

The UK and Liechtenstein have also agreed a tax arrangement that allows British investors in Liechtenstein to declare their undeclared income and gains held in Liechtenstein voluntarily until 2015. This has since been extended until 5 April 2016. The benefit of disclosing under the facility is that there will be substantially reduced penalties.

Living in Liechtenstein

As far as living there is concerned, Liechtenstein is very scenic, with some beautiful mountains and valleys. It's warm in summer but there's plenty of snow in winter. The cost of living is notoriously high.

As it's not part of the EU you'll need to get a residence permit if you want to live there. Although it's part of the European Economic Area (EEA), given its small size, residence permits are restricted.

Currently 28 residence permits are issued each year to employed persons and eight per year to non-employed persons.

MALTA

Malta is situated in the Mediterranean, just below Sicily. It's not a well-known bolthole but offers some excellent tax breaks to individuals who want to establish themselves in a flexible low-tax haven 'on the cheap'.

The actual income-tax rates are quite high, with all but the lowest-paid facing a marginal tax rate of 35%.

However, Malta has become a popular tax haven because it has special tax rules to attract skilled and wealthy expats.

Expats Working in Malta

The 2011 Highly Qualified Persons Rules allow certain expats working in Malta to be subject to a flat tax rate of 15% on their employment income.

You must have a minimum income of €75,000 per year (excluding fringe benefits and discretionary bonuses). This is adjusted for the increase in the retail price index and means that for 2014 the minimum income is €81,000. Any excess over €5 million would be tax free.

Eligible jobs are those with companies licensed or recognised by the Malta Financial Services Authority in the following posts:

- Chief executive officer, chief risk officer, chief financial officer, chief operations officer, chief technology officer.
- Portfolio manager, chief investment officer, senior trader, senior analyst, actuarial professional, chief underwriting officer, chief insurance technical officer.
- Head of marketing, head of investor relations.

The 15% tax rate applies for five years for EEA national and Swiss nationals and four years for everyone else.

For more information:

www.ird.gov.mt/taxguides/qualifiedpersons.aspx

High Net Worth Individuals Scheme

This scheme replaced the old "Permanent Residence Scheme" and is designed to attract well-off non-working retired expats. The old scheme was suspended in December 2010 and the new High Net Worth Individuals Scheme applies for 2011 onwards.

The main benefit is a 15% income tax rate on overseas income remitted to Malta (foreign income that is not remitted is tax free).

However, the new rules are much less attractive than the old rules.

The rules require a minimum tax payment of €20,000 and this is increased by €2,500 for each dependant. There is also a one-off €6,000 administrative fee to apply for this special tax status (non refundable).

You also have to either purchase a Maltese property for at least €400,000 or rent a property for at least €20,000 per year.

Maltese General Tax law

EU nationals have the right to reside in Malta and can make use of some very favourable tax rules if they are non-domiciled:

- Only overseas income actually arising or remitted to Malta is taxed (at up to 35%). There is no minimum amount of income that has to be remitted so you could live off capital tax free.

- Overseas capital gains can be remitted tax free.

There is also no inheritance tax, gift tax or wealth tax.

All in all, Malta looks like a good rival to some of the other European low-tax havens such as Cyprus and the Isle of Man.

Malta Double Tax Treaties

Malta has a fair number of double tax treaties, which can help to ensure that overseas income is only taxed in Malta.

The agreement with the UK, for example, can help to ensure that UK pensions are not subject to any tax in the UK and are taxed in Malta, potentially at just 15%. So Malta could be an attractive retirement destination.

Business Taxation

Malta does not have a separate corporate tax system. Companies are subject to income tax at the top marginal rate of 35%. However, the so-called imputation system ensures that the effective corporate tax rate is reduced to approximately 5%.

Malta has a big network of double tax treaties (including treaties with all EU members), which means it could be a good location for your business.

In terms of exchange of information treaties, Malta is on the OECD 'white list' and has signed numerous exchange of information agreements.

Living in Malta

The standard of living is very high with good schools and medical facilities (ranked fifth in the world by the World Health Organisation). The University of Malta has an excellent reputation and is open to the children of permanent residents.

The island boasts an excellent Mediterranean lifestyle, with good restaurants and golf resorts. The all-important crime rate is still very low, and you'll find plenty of locals leave their doors open, even when they go out.

Whilst Malta has a high standard of living, the cost of living is surprisingly low – lower than, for example, the UK, Spain, Portugal, France, Italy and Cyprus.

Property in Malta

Initial property buying costs include stamp duty at 5%, notary fees of 1%, and legal fees of 1%.

There are no property taxes payable in Malta.

If you own a property and occupied it for at least three consecutive years immediately preceding the date of transfer, and as long as the property is transferred within 12 months from when you vacate the premises, the transfer is tax free. According to the Income Tax Act, "own residence" must be a dwelling house which is your only or principal residence.

Demand for property in Malta has improved in recent months, pushing prices higher.

You can find properties to rent or buy on these websites:

- **www.remax-malta.com**
- **www.maltahomes.net**
- **www.rightmove.co.uk**
- **www.franksalt.com.mt**

Overall, Malta offers excellent benefits and should be given serious consideration by anyone wanting to live in a country with low tax rates and a Mediterranean way of life.

MONACO

Located on the stunning French Riviera, there is probably no tax haven more famous than Monaco.

In recent years the well-known British entrepreneur Philip Green has made full use of the favourable tax laws there to pay his Monaco-based wife hundreds of millions of pounds in tax-free dividends from UK companies.

There is no income tax or capital gains tax in Monaco – the main tax is a business profits tax that is levied on certain companies (but most expats structure their affairs so as to avoid it).

There is also inheritance tax but there are two major exemptions that limit its application in practice. Firstly, the tax is payable only on assets situated in Monaco and secondly the tax rate depends on how closely related the parties are. The closer the relationship, the lower the inheritance tax rate.

The rates payable are as follows:

	Tax Rate
Wife, parents and children	0%
Brothers and sisters	8%
Uncles, aunts, nieces and nephews	10%
Other relatives	13%
Unrelated persons	16%

So assets left to a spouse or children can usually be transferred free of inheritance tax.

Monaco is well known as a playground of the rich and famous. It has gorgeous weather, exclusive shops and hotels and is a fantastically safe place to live.

Not only is there a large police force (something like one policeman for every 100 residents) but the entire principality is covered by CCTV.

As you would expect, the standard of living is extremely high but so are living costs – you'll be looking at paying over £50 for just two cocktails in one of the swanky bars.

Buying a property in Monaco is simple in theory as no restrictions are placed on non-residents.

In practice most of the decent properties are far too expensive for the average expat. A recent survey of EU property prices found it has the highest property prices in the whole of Europe.

Most of the residents live in apartments and the best of these go for several million Euros. I recently saw one studio flat going for around €1 million – not a great solution for a couple with young children but possibly worth considering if you're free and single.

If you're after a decent villa or house in the principality, brace yourself for open-wallet surgery. You could end up paying as much as €35 million.

The real attraction of Monaco as a tax haven is its geographic location and lifestyle. Unlike many tax havens that are situated in the middle of nowhere, Monaco is only a short drive from several major European cities.

Access to banks and financial services is excellent, as you would expect given the number of mega-rich inhabitants.

Obtaining residence in Monaco is not as difficult as you might expect, provided you have sufficient assets and income.

There are basically three ways you can get a residence permit: by establishing a business in Monaco, by becoming an employee of a Monaco company or by retiring there.

For most wealthy immigrants, this last category is the most relevant one, as it applies to anyone who is not going to be involved in a trading or business activity.

If you are an EU resident, to obtain a residence permit (carte de séjour) you have to apply to the Foreign Residents Section of Monaco's Sûreté Publique. You'll need to show evidence of accommodation (for example, a lease or title deeds to a property) and proof of your financial standing (for example, a bank reference).

Applications take one to two months. If you're successful you'll get a residence permit, which is initially valid for 12 months. If you're not an EU resident, the process is only slightly more complex as you'll first need to get a visa, which more or less involves the same requirements as getting a residence permit.

While there is no personal income tax in Monaco (except for French nationals in certain circumstances), companies established in Monaco have to, in theory, pay a business profits tax at a rate of around 33% after five years of trading (during the first years they pay tax at a lower rate, which increases annually on a sliding scale).

In practice there are, however, a number of exceptions to the business profits tax, including:

• Businesses that are not involved in holding intellectual property or in certain trading activities (this would exempt telecommuters).
• Businesses that are involved in industrial and commercial activities, 75% or more of whose income comes from within Monaco, and
• Non-resident entities in any line of business. Residence is determined by the residence of the directors, shareholders and the location of board meetings.

If you set up a business and employ staff in Monaco there will be national insurance to pay, which is relatively high, with the employer on average paying 35% of salaries as social security payments.

There are no withholding taxes in the principality.

Monaco does permit the use of trusts, however these can only be established by Monaco residents.

Following pressure from the international community, Monaco has agreed to follow the OECD Exchange of Information Treaty and to implement an EU anti-fraud agreement to allow it to exchange information on all tax matters with all European Union member states that are signatories to the agreement.

Overall, however, Monaco is an excellent choice for very wealthy expats who want to live in the heart of Europe and pay no tax (although some may regard the lifestyle as a bit 'Footballers' Wives').

Monaco on a Budget?

Helped by new rules for residency in Andorra, Monaco can be as inexpensive as its main competitor in Europe with a distinct advantage of being close to the European transport system, including the rail network and an international airport.

With Andorra requiring a 400,000 Euro minimum investment in government bonds or buying an Andorra property to that value, or a mix of the two, how can Monaco compete to attract those looking for a tax haven in Europe?

The answer lies in how the applicant approaches residency and property in Monaco, and how long he or she needs a tax haven for.

Given that many of those wanting to move to a low tax jurisdiction only need it for five or six years before they can return home the answer is in renting, and choosing one of the Monaco banks that takes a low initial deposit to secure a certificate showing that the applicant has sufficent funds to be able to look after themselves financially.

A one bedroom apartment in a relatively good building with Mediterranean views and a parking space will cost around 3,000 Euros a month - for two bedrooms the current rentals start at around 5,000 Euros a month.

Part of being accepted as a Monaco resident is showing the ability to support yourself financially, and this is done by getting a certificate from one of the Monaco banks showing that a deposit has been made.

Different banks ask for various amounts, and these can vary widely from bank to bank, but one of the leading ones is able to produce the certificate with a deposit of 100,000 Euros.

So for someone wanting Monaco residency the overall cost of renting a one bedroom apartment for five years would be 180,000 Euros plus 100,000 deposit for the bank (which the applicant keeps).

Or for a two bedroom apartment 300,000 Euros, again plus a 100,000 Euros deposit which is returnable when residency is rescinded.

PANAMA

Located in Central America, close to Costa Rica, Panama is one of the most popular and established tax havens around. Its popularity is thanks not just to the offshore companies and foundations on offer but also because those 'in the know' regard it as a good place to live.

Panama's tax advantages stem from the fact that it has a territorial tax system. This means that income that does not arise in Panama is not subject to tax in Panama. Only Panama-source income is taxed.

In fact you'll find that quite a few of the Central and South American countries do not tax any of your overseas income or gains. This makes countries such as Costa Rica, Panama, Uruguay, Nicaragua, Paraguay, Guatemala and Bolivia tax efficient for anyone who is not earning any locally derived income.

Unfortunately not all of them apply this territorial basis and, for example, Brazil, Peru, Ecuador, Chile, Mexico, Colombia and Venezuela could still tax you in full on your worldwide earnings, so you need to be careful.

This rule applies to both personal and corporate income. So income tax is only payable on income from a business carried on within Panama or by individuals employed there.

The tax year is the same as the calendar year, ending on December 31.

An individual is resident in Panama if he or she spends more than 183 days in the country in a calendar year.

In Panama, income tax, where it applies, is levied as follows: the first US$11,000 is exempt and a 15% rate applies to income up to US$50,000. Income over US$50,000 is taxed at 25%.

Individuals are entitled to a US$800 basic deduction (joint tax return). Mortgage interest up to US$15,000 per year is tax deductible, as are medical expenses incurred in Panama and not covered by insurance.

Capital gains tax is levied at 10% on Panama-source capital gains.

There is no inheritance tax or wealth tax.

There is, however, a 9% social security contribution payable by employees on their remuneration.

There is also a real property tax, which ranges from 1.75% to 2.1%.

Company Tax

In terms of asset protection, Panama has agreed to implement the Exchange of Information Treaty. Panama is popular as a corporate tax haven for a number of reasons.

Its International Business Company (IBC) and foundation structures are often promoted by offshore incorporators as effective tax-avoidance tools (although, and I can't reiterate this enough, you should pay little attention to most of these advisers and get detailed advice on your *home country's* anti-avoidance and other offshore legislation).

Panama also offers good value for money and, while not being the cheapest location for offshore company formation, is certainly significantly cheaper than the more expensive jurisdictions such as Bermuda. For example, you can set up an IBC for less than $1,500, whereas in Bermuda an offshore company could cost you four times as much.

Panama is also known for its strong maritime business and good privacy laws. Political stability is also recognized as good.

As banking and shipping are Panama's two main 'offshore' industries there is a good selection of banks to choose from (more than 140). Panamanian bank accounts are becoming more popular because interest is tax free and, for EU nationals, they are excluded from the Savings Tax Directive.

Companies are subject to the territorial tax rule, just as individuals are. Therefore, provided a company doesn't derive its income from Panamanian activities, there will be no tax payable.

This means that, as a location for offshore IBCs, Panama offers a sound 0% tax regime in most cases. This, allied to the significant privacy benefits, makes it a very popular destination.

Living in Panama

Aside from the tax benefits, Panama is a popular retirement destination due to its low cost of living (some say you can live comfortably on $1,200 per month) and because it is more developed than most people expect it to be.

It has modern infrastructure and high-quality health care, e.g. the Johns Hopkins-affiliated Punta Pacifica Hospital, which is one of the most sophisticated in Latin America. Health insurance is cheaper than in the US (there aren't as many frivolous lawsuits).

Panama is also a relatively safe place to live (the world-famous Pinkerton's Detective Agency listed Panama as the safest place to live in all of the Americas).

Although the climate is tropical, Panama lies outside the hurricane belt.

Becoming Resident in Panama

There are special programmes to attract foreigners to move to the country under the Pensionado Program.

You'll qualify provided you have a minimum pension of US$750 per month and invest at least US$100,000 in property. Alternatively you must have a minimum income of US$1,000 per month (no real estate commitment), plus US$250 per dependant.

You will then be entitled to Panamanian residency and will be entitled to a number of special discounts including:

- 50% off entertainment (e.g. movies, sporting events)
- 30% off bus, boat, and train fares
- 25% off airline tickets
- Up to 50% off hotels
- Up to 20% off uninsured medical bills
- 20% off professional services

Pensionados also receive a one-time exemption on the importation of household goods worth up to US$10,000.

Two words of warning about the Pensionado Program:

- A lot is made of the special discounts in the expat media but you may not be able to enjoy some of them in practice (e.g. some are already factored into the price, some may simply be refused and some may be downright awkward to claim, for example at restaurants).

- There are many emigration consultants charging fat fees to help people make Pensionado applications – be careful about parting with your cash.

Person of Means Visa

This is designed for those who wish to live in Panama off their own means, without the need or desire to work or start a business.

The requirements are as follows:

- Deposit US$300,000 for three years in a Panama bank, or
- Invest US$300,000 in real estate, or
- A combination of the above

Panama Property

Property prices in Panama surged between 2004 and 2007, as American buyers poured in. The market crashed when the easy money dried up during the credit crisis. There is now a glut of condos and prices of some waterfront units have fallen from US$280,000 to under US$200,000.

You can pick up apartments in Panama City for as little as US$60,000 and homes in the countryside for as little as US$50,000.

SEYCHELLES

The Seychelles has long been recognised as one of the world's most popular tax havens, particularly in terms of using low-cost offshore companies. But is this still the case?

The Seychelles is seen as beneficial because of the absence of many taxes. In particular there is:

- No capital gains tax
- No gift or estate taxes
- A system of territorial taxation

The territorial system simply means that only locally sourced income is taxed.

Note that the territorial system is different to the remittance basis because under the territorial basis overseas income and gains are exempt from tax, even if remitted into the Seychelles.

Note that the Seychelles is not subject to the EU Savings Directive.

Taxes that are levied include:

- Import duties
- VAT
- Business taxes

Business taxes will apply to income from self-employment either as a sole proprietor or partnership. Business taxes will also apply to rental income from Seychelles property.

Rates of business tax are high with a top rate of 33%. Remember, however, that foreign-source income, even foreign-source business income is not taxable.

Even taking these taxes into account the Seychelles can therefore be very attractive to UK emigrants.

UK dividends as well as non-Seychelles business income could be completely free of Seychelles taxes if you established residence there.

So for many owners of internet businesses, the exemption for foreign source income could be extremely beneficial.

Income Tax Reintroduced

A personal income tax was reintroduced in 2010, over 20 years after it was abolished in favour of social security contributions.

The personal income tax system replaces the Social Security Fund (SSF) contributions now paid by employers and employees.

As of 1st January 2011, the personal income tax rate is a flat 15%, although it only applies to employees. Employers pay tax at 20% on the value of benefits (eg car or living accommodation) that they provide to employees.

Obtaining a Residence Permit

If you want to go and live there you would usually need to acquire a residence permit. You are eligible to be granted one if you are not a prohibited immigrant to the country, have a family or a connection with the Seychelles domestically and have made or will still make a contribution that will greatly help the growth of the social, economic and cultural life of the country.

As a holder of a residence permit, you would need to live in the Seychelles for at least five days every year. You would also have to provide proof of your financial status by providing a bank guarantee and bringing at least SR100,000 per year (£4,600 approximately) into the country.

The fee for the residence permit is SR150,000 (around £7,000) for the main applicant and SR75,000 for your spouse and SR25,000 for children.

Company Taxation

Aside from actually moving there, the Seychelles is very popular for offshore company incorporation. In particular, companies are completely exempt from all taxes on income derived outside the Seychelles.

A big bonus is that it's still relatively cheap to set up a Seychelles IBC. For instance, I've seen Seychelles IBC packages for just $800.

The new proposals don't mention any changes to the tax position of Seychelles IBCs and provided this continues to be the case there should still be strong demand.

An increasingly important Seychelles company 'advantage' is the fact that Seychelles is an independent country.

It is not seen as a British 'possession' (such as BVI, Anguilla, Turks & Caicos, the Cayman Islands, the Isle of Man and the Channel Islands). These jurisdictions are suffering from excessive regulatory tightening as a result of EU policy (which they are required to implement).

If you're looking to move overseas to avoid tax, the Seychelles may not be top of the list until more detail is available on the nature of some of the recent tax changes. In terms of establishing an offshore IBC, however, it is likely to remain very popular.

SINGAPORE

Singapore is becoming increasingly important as one of the low-tax havens and is keen to attract Westerners. It's a good choice if you're looking to dispose of assets, because there is no capital gains tax. In addition, Singapore does not levy a withholding tax on dividends. Interest and royalties paid to non-residents are, however, subject to a 10% or 15% withholding tax.

Singapore is, therefore, not completely tax free but, like Panama and Costa Rica, it applies the territorial basis of taxation. Therefore, even if you become a tax resident of Singapore you can avoid paying income tax on your overseas pension or investment income.

The city state has also benefited from the introduction of the European Savings Tax Directive. As Singapore is outside the scope of the directive it has seen a sudden rush of cash into its banks by EU residents, keen to keep their money away from the prying eyes of governments.

Following international pressure Singapore has signed up to implement the OECD Exchange of Information agreement and is now on the OECD white list.

Singapore uses one of the standard methods of assessing residence and if you have your permanent home there or spend more than half of the tax year there, you'll be classed as a resident. As a resident individual you'll only be taxed on income derived from Singapore. Residents are taxed at graduated rates, ranging from 2% to 20%.

If you're not a tax resident of Singapore you'll also only be taxed on income that is actually derived from Singapore. In most cases this will just be local employment income. In terms of tax rates there is either a flat rate of 15 per cent, without the benefit of any personal reliefs, or the residents' graduated rates (whichever is higher).

Singapore has concluded double-taxation agreements with over 60 countries, which could come in handy if you need to establish residence overseas but still want to visit your home country. In this case, provided you establish residence in Singapore both under their tax rules and under the 'tiebreaker' clause in the treaty, you should be able to avoid being a tax resident in your 'home' country.

In terms of company tax, the tax residence status of a company in Singapore depends on the usual test of where the management control of the business is exercised. If you use a Singapore resident company, it will be taxed on any income accruing in Singapore or income that is received in Singapore from overseas.

There is a special rule for overseas dividends that mainly affects Singapore holding companies. This states that there is a tax exemption for the overseas dividends, provided they are not remitted into Singapore and:

- The highest corporate tax rate of the country from where the income is received is at least 15%, and
- The income has already been taxed in the overseas country.

Singapore companies also enjoy some very attractive tax breaks. The current corporation tax rate is 17% with the following exemptions:

- 75% exemption for the first SG$10,000 of chargeable income, and
- 50% exemption for the next SG$290,000 of chargeable income.

Effective corporate tax rates are therefore as follows:

Chargeable income	Effective tax rate
First $10,000	4.25%
Next $290,000	8.5%
In excess of $300,000	17%

New companies are exempt from tax on the first SG$100,000 and on 50% of the next SG$200,000 of taxable income for the first three years.

Residence in Singapore

There are a few different options for individuals who want to obtain a residence permit to live in Singapore. Most expats would probably do so under either an employment pass or as an investor under the Global Investor Programme.

The Singaporean authorities state that to qualify under the investor category you can either:

- Invest at least SG$2.5 million in a new business entity or expansion of an existing business operation
- Invest at least SG$2.5 million in a GIP-approved fund

For more information go to:
www.contactsingapore.org.sg/investors/move/global_investor_programme

There are also schemes that allow skilled foreigners and professionals to qualify as permanent residents.

Another option is the EntrePass scheme. This allows entrepreneurs that form a Singapore company to qualify for a special employment pass that also provides a resident visa. The new company must have SG$50,000 or more in paid-up capital.

Singapore Property

Housing in Singapore is expensive. The most basic one-bedroom apartments start at over £400,000, although even these tend to be in exclusive, high-quality developments.

Foreigners looking to buy property are subject to some restrictions. It used to be the case that you could only buy apartments or condominiums in buildings of six storeys or more. However this restriction was lifted in 2005 and such property can now be purchased by foreigners without prior Government approval.

However, if you are looking to buy landed property such as houses, bungalows or land plots in the country, you need to seek approval from the SLA (Singapore Land Authority).

Such properties come with a large price tag. A luxury five-bedroom house with stunning views and private pool will cost upwards of £10,000,000.

With such high purchase prices, it's no wonder that many foreigners choose to rent their accommodation. Monthly rents start at £1,000 for studio apartments but climb very steeply for more rooms or a more desirable location.

In summary, Singapore can offer good opportunities for both personal residence and company incorporation.

Provided you obtain income from overseas and can take full advantage of the territorial basis of taxation, Singapore is an attractive tax haven with a very high standard of living.

ST KITTS & NEVIS

St Kitts and Nevis is a federation of two tiny volcanic islands in the eastern Caribbean with a population of just 43,000.

The islands were discovered by Columbus in 1493 and settled by the British in the 17th century, finally becoming independent in 1983.

The climate is tropical but with a steady cool breeze for most of the year. Crime is low and tends to be restricted to purse snatching and other petty offences.

The islands are a popular tourist destination, thanks to an abundance of pristine beaches. However, if you're looking for a place to settle, you would have to get used to the isolation.

There are very few shops and you would probably have to go to nearby St Martin to buy any luxury goods. St Kitts and Nevis levies import duties and the overall cost of living is high. Importing a car, for example, will set you back over 50% in import duties.

The islands have good transport links, with flights to the UK and US as well as other key destinations. The main language is English.

As for tax, St Kitts and Nevis is one of the 'no-tax' havens and is becoming increasingly popular for personal offshore tax planning. The islands offer good privacy protection (which is one of the reasons St Kitts is popular in asset protection strategies) and it doesn't cost very much to set up an offshore company there.

There is no personal income tax, although domestic companies face a corporation tax rate of 35%. Although this is an extremely high tax rate, there is specific legislation that exempts offshore companies, as long as they only do business with non-residents. There is, however, a 10% withholding tax in operation for certain payments overseas.

If you work on the islands you also have to pay social security but the rates are very low – just 5% of your monthly earnings up to an earnings ceiling of $2,500 per month.

There is no capital gains tax on St Kitts and Nevis except when you sell local assets which you've owned for less than 12 months.

The fact that the islands are not a crown dependency may also be beneficial as it means they are not subject to the EU Savings Tax Directive.

This gives St Kitts an advantage over other UK dependencies in the Caribbean and over traditional UK offshore centres such as the Channel Islands.

The island has agreed to implement the OECD Exchange of Information Treaty and to date has signed over 12 such agreements.

If you want to invest in property you will have to obtain an Alien Land Holding Licence. There's also stamp duty to pay and your total purchase costs could add an extra 15% to the price.

Once a year the rental value of your property is assessed and a 5% house tax has to be paid on this rental value, although it's unlikely you would ever end up paying more than $1,000.

The good news is that all your rental income is tax free and there is no capital gains tax unless you sell your property within one year.

Property is less expensive than many other islands in the Caribbean. One-bedroom apartments start at £200,000 and stunning two-bedroom villas with spectacular views start at £370,000 in recently built complexes. If you're not afraid to get your hands dirty, £557,000 can buy a large plantation house with grounds in need of complete renovation – a great investment opportunity.

If you want to obtain a residence permit you have to complete an application form that asks for some personal details and how you intend to support yourself while living on the islands. You also have to submit evidence of your assets and a variety of other documents.

For more information go to:

http://www.stkittsnevis.org/visainfo.html

Another reason St Kitts and Nevis is so popular is that it effectively allows you to buy citizenship and a passport.

There are a number of conditions that have to be satisfied (for example, they'll want proof that you don't have a criminal record).

The most important requirement is that you invest at least $400,000 ($350,000 before 2012) in an 'approved investment project', which includes certain properties.

The Government also requires a registration fee ($50,000 for the main applicant and a further $25,000 for your spouse and each child under 18).

For more information visit: http://www.ciu.gov.kn/

If you want to establish permanent residence overseas quickly and perhaps even lose your UK domicile status, obtaining citizenship in St Kitts and Nevis may be useful.

SWITZERLAND

Swiss banks are the most famous in the world and have an excellent reputation for confidentiality.

As with many European countries, Switzerland taxes its residents on their worldwide income and the tax rates vary according to which district or 'canton' you live in. The lowest tax cantons are Zug, Schwyz, Nidwald and Zurich.

Tax rates can be as high as 35%, which does not compare favourably with other tax havens but Switzerland is not really a tax haven in the conventional sense of the word.

Foreign individuals can drastically reduce their tax bills by taking advantage of what's known as the 'Fiscal Deal'. Essentially, this is a tax deal that also comes with a residence permit.

In early 2012 the Swiss Senate confirmed that the Fiscal Deal will still be available although some Cantons (eg Zurich) have abolished it.

The Swiss authorities are very picky about who can take advantage of this tax-saving opportunity – you'll only be able to take advantage of these tax breaks if you are prepared to become a resident, don't intend working or running a business from Switzerland and aren't a Swiss national.

You'll need to discuss the details with the particular canton in which you want to live and they'll tell you how your taxable income will be calculated.

A common assessment would be to have your taxable income calculated as a multiple of your property's rental value. The rental value is simply the amount an owner would pay for renting a similar property.

From 2012 the Fiscal Deal rules have been tightened up so that the minimum taxable income will be seven times the annual rental value of the residence, instead of five. For those living in a hotel, it will be the equivalent of three times their annual boarding and food costs instead of two.

In order to apply for the Fiscal Deal you'll need to be worth not less than two million Swiss Francs (around £1.4 million).

Just as with the Gibraltar HNWI scheme, the tax rates payable under this system are the same as would apply normally – it's just that the amount of taxable income is restricted to a much lower level.

The drawback (aside from the minimum net wealth requirement) is that you would not be able to work or run a business in Switzerland. Fine if you're independently wealthy but not so great if you still have to earn a living.

The Fiscal Deal is a famous part of the Swiss tax system and has been used by many famous people to avoid tax, including the French singer, Johnny Hallyday. He was being taxed at rates of up to 72% in France and left there to become a resident of Gstaad in Switzerland. He has since then sought Belgian citizenship and hopes to eventually move to Monaco (after having lost his French citizenship).

Other famous people who have taken advantage of the Fiscal Deal include Phil Collins, Tina Turner, Michael Schumacher and Boris Becker.

The qualifying income requirements vary from canton to canton.

In addition to the income taxes the Swiss have:

- A transfer or property appreciation tax on property disposals that can be 5%.
- Social security, which can be pretty high if you are an employee (roughly 10%), although this doesn't affect residents under the Fiscal Deal as they're not allowed to gain employment in any case.
- Inheritance tax is levied by some of the cantons, so if you want to avoid or minimize IHT you need to be flexible as to where you live (for example, the canton of Schwyz does not charge any inheritance tax and many of the others don't charge inheritance tax on transfers to spouses and children).
- A wealth tax, levied by the cantons, payable by residents on the value of assets in Switzerland (often at a rate of 1.5%).

It should be noted that the Swiss canton of Zurich has eliminated the flat-rate tax model so that foreigners are now taxed on the basis of income and subject to the usual income tax rates. This does not, however, affect many of the other cantons, which still offer the flat rate tax/fiscal deal.

Tax issues aside, Switzerland offers an enviable lifestyle in the heart of

Europe. The property prices, while certainly not low, are reasonable and far cheaper than many parts of London. Crime is low and the climate is mild in many parts of the country.

However, you must be prepared to pay for the privilege of being a Swiss resident as the cost of living is high (among the highest in Europe, along with Norway and Iceland).

In terms of corporate tax, a company is deemed to be resident in Switzerland if it is either incorporated in Switzerland or effectively managed from there (a similar rule to the UK).

Resident companies have to pay tax on their worldwide income, however non-resident companies only pay tax on profits generated from property and permanent establishments located in Switzerland. The tax rates vary from canton to canton but can be as low as 12%. It came third in a 2007 survey for the best overall corporate tax regime in Europe (after Cyprus and Ireland).

As you'd expect, the Swiss take banking secrecy very seriously and although Switzerland does exchange information with other tax authorities, this will only be done when there is a case of serious tax fraud or evasion.

Switzerland has watered down its information exchange policies after pressure in 2008 and following the 2009 G20 summit. However, the country is making efforts to retain bank secrecy and ruling out automatic exchange of information. Instead, foreign authorities will need to approach Switzerland with the names of the suspected tax evaders.

If you're looking at having one of the famous Swiss bank accounts, you should read Chapter 9 on the impact of the European Savings Tax Directive.

TURKS & CAICOS ISLANDS

The Turks and Caicos is made up of 45 islands and cays located south-east of the Bahamas. The total population is less than 25,000, most of whom live on Providenciales (Provo), the biggest of the islands.

The Turks and Caicos is a British overseas territory (much like many of the other Caribbean tax havens) and enjoys self-rule under a Governor and elected council.

As you'd expect, the official language is English and the legal system is derived largely from English law. The economy is dependent on financial services and tourism (miles of coral reefs and white beaches).

Crime is very low and the infrastructure is generally good with broadband internet access and a good but expensive telephone service.
There are direct flights to the US and Canada.

The Turks and Caicos offers the same tax benefits as many of the other Caribbean tax havens. There is no:

- Income tax
- Capital gains tax
- Inheritance tax

The Government raises money through indirect taxes such as import duties and stamp duty (which ranges from 0% to almost 10%). They were planning to introduce VAT in 2013 but this has been scrapped.

The Turks and Caicos has strict banking confidentiality laws and the unauthorized disclosure of confidential information is a crime.

While there is a treaty in place with the US allowing for the exchange of information relating to serious criminal offences, tax matters are specifically excluded from the ambit of the treaty.

Note that as a UK crown dependency the Turks and Caicos is implementing the EU Savings Tax Directive and implementing a withholding tax for EU residents.

This may make it a less attractive tax haven than other countries in the region, such as Panama, Antigua and the Bahamas, all of which are not currently bound by the provisions of the directive.

It is, however, on the OECD 'white list' and has signed a number of exchange of information treaties.

Property prices vary enormously and prime beachfront villas can cost around $2.5 million. However, you can pick up a one-acre parcel of land for around $75,000 or a beachfront plot for as little as $200,000. I've seen a beachfront house with 150 feet of ocean frontage going for $495,000 and one-bedroom apartments for as little as $200,000.

At the other end of the scale, the islands have some truly outstanding luxury properties. One 10-bedroom villa with wonderful sea views and an outlook on the marina is currently on the market for just over $25,000,000!

Because of the necessity to import practically everything, the cost of living on the islands is comparatively high.

If you're looking to emigrate there permanently you could consider obtaining a Permanent Residence Certificate. In order to obtain one you would need to make an investment in local property or a local business.

The minimum investment required is $500,000 on Providenciales and $125,000 on the other islands. However, prior to making an investment you can obtain a temporary residence permit for three years before transferring to the permanent residence scheme. As a resident you can also enter and leave TCI as you please.

There was a temporary hold on applications under this scheme in early 2010 due to a backlog of applications.

If you want to work on the Turks and Caicos islands you need a work permit. As with other Caribbean countries they are careful to preserve jobs for locals, so you need to have special skills.

There are a number of different corporate entities you can set up including an International Business Company (IBC), limited partnership, hybrid company or trust. As you'd expect, there is no tax levied on any of these. In fact, when you form an IBC you'll automatically receive a certificate of tax exemption for a period of 20 years. This is a guarantee that the authorities won't change their minds and implement a corporate tax on income or gains during the 20-year period.

Therefore the Turks and Caicos, along with other Caribbean jurisdictions, offer a tax-free lifestyle and straightforward residency requirements both for individuals and companies.

UNITED STATES

Certainly not a traditional tax haven by any stretch of the imagination, the US does offer some specific tax-saving opportunities.

In particular, a US limited liability company (LLC) is often a useful tool in international tax planning.

This is because LLCs that carry on no business in the US and derive no income from any sources within the US may not need to file a US federal tax return.

An LLC is a cross between a partnership and a company. It provides the benefit of limited liability that a company offers but also gives the 'pass through taxation' benefits of a partnership (the profits can be taxed in the hands of the partners instead of in the company).

In other words, the tax status of the LLC would depend on the residence of its members. For US tax purposes non-US individuals trading outside the US via an LLC would therefore not be liable to pay US tax on the LLC's profits.

The US can therefore be a useful intermediary for foreign business and investments. In particular, one of the benefits is access to the US's wide tax treaty network.

We'll take a closer look at the uses to which offshore companies can be put in Chapter 6. However, a good use for a US LLC may be as part of a re-invoicing strategy. This involves interposing an LLC between a trader and a customer and, in effect, diverting a proportion of the profit to the LLC. The payments would be made in exchange for the LLC providing services to the trading company (for example, administrative services).

LLCs can be set up in many of the US states, however the favoured states are Delaware or Nevada as these offer the best tax options as well as minimal administrative requirements.

If you did set up a US LLC, it would not need to file a US tax return or pay US income tax provided any trade in question was carried on outside the US.

DENMARK

Although Denmark is generally accepted as being one of the most expensive and overtaxed countries in the world, it does offer a number of tax-saving benefits to the astute non-resident.

The most popular strategy is setting up a zero-tax holding company. Some of the big international conglomerates such as Pepsico do this.

There are a few conditions that need to be satisfied to obtain this zero-tax status but these are not difficult to satisfy and the benefits more than outweigh the inconvenience of jumping through a few hoops.

The advantage of using Denmark is that it has a substantial number of double tax treaties with other countries (over 60). This makes it an ideal place to establish a holding company as this allows dividends to be transferred from subsidiaries based in various parts of the world without any tax being deducted. See Chapter 7 on holding companies for more details of the advantages of Danish holding companies.

UNITED KINGDOM

Again, not your traditional tax haven but the UK has some very useful tax laws that can be exploited by astute individuals.

In particular, the domicile rules allow foreign persons to live in the UK and pay no tax on their overseas income and capital gains, provided these amounts are not remitted to the UK.

The benefit of these 'remittance rules' has, however, been significantly reduced recently. Proposals that have applied since 6th April 2008 mean that, once a foreigner has been resident in the UK for more than seven of the past ten tax years, they can only avoid UK tax by keeping income abroad if they pay an annual £30,000 tax charge to the UK tax authorities.

As of 6th April 2012 this charge has been raised to £50,000 for non-domiciliaries who have been UK resident for at least 12 years. This is unlikely to put off the very wealthy from moving to the UK but anyone with more modest overseas income or capital gains would need to consider whether it's worthwhile claiming the remittance basis.

In terms of business entities, the UK has introduced a relatively new type of business structure known as the Limited Liability Partnership (LLP). If certain circumstances are met, the LLP can effectively operate free of any UK tax.

To all intents and purposes, the British LLP is comparable to a United States LLC: it is a combination of a standard limited liability company and a partnership.

Just like limited companies, LLPs provide limited liability to members (in contrast to partnerships where partners' liability is unlimited). However, LLPs are still treated as partnerships as far as taxation is concerned and tax is assessed individually on each member after the distribution of the LLP's profits among them. The LLP, as such, is not taxed at all.

The legislation requires that an LLP has at least two members. They may be of any nationality and need not be UK residents.

In fact, provided the LLP members are located outside the United Kingdom and no business is conducted with or within the UK, the LLP has no liability for UK taxation. For a UK non-resident, an LLP is an excellent addition to a collection of 'non-offshore' yet tax-free corporate entities. Other reasons why the UK is regarded as a tax haven by many include:

• Whilst the top rate of income tax for UK residents is currently 45%, capital gains tax is levied at 18% to 28%. Entrepreneurs Relief can result in a 10% tax rate for sales of many businesses and shareholdings. The lifetime limit on capital gains that can qualify for Entrepreneurs Relief has been increased to £10 million per person.

• Non-residents aren't subject to capital gains tax even if the assets disposed of are in the UK, unless they are used in a UK trade. There are very few other developed EU countries that adopt this rule. Most tax gains on assets located within their borders. Note that the UK tax authorities are consulting on changes to make sales of UK residential property by non UK residents subject to UK CGT.

• The UK offers a highly attractive tax regime for offshore trusts made by settlors who are non-resident and non-domiciled. In this case foreign income and any gains arising to the trust (including gains arising on a disposal of UK assets) aren't subject to tax. In addition, non-resident beneficiaries won't be taxed on distributions from the trust.

• The UK doesn't levy withholding tax on outgoing dividends.

• Corporation tax rates are 20% for small companies and 21% for larger companies from April 2014.

• The sale by a UK holding company of shares in its trading subsidiaries (provided the conditions for 'substantial shareholding relief' are met) will be exempt from UK tax.

• The UK has a very good network of double tax treaties and also has the added advantage that it's not featured on any tax haven 'blacklists'.

LABUAN

Labuan is a small East Malaysian island in the South China Sea. In 1990 the Malaysian Government set it up as an International Offshore Financial Centre.

It's fair to say that Labuan has remained a fairly low-key tax haven, attractive for those wishing to keep out of the spotlight.

Offshore Trading Companies in Labuan pay 3% tax on profits or a fixed sum of RM20,000 (around $5,000), whichever is lower. If you form an investment or non-trading company you won't pay any tax at all.

If privacy is important, the company can simply elect to pay the maximum tax of RM20,000 per annum and there would then be no need to file accounts.

New provisions in 2008 allow offshore trading companies to elect to be subject to standard Malaysian tax rules. This would then allow access to Malaysia's double tax treaty network (over 60) as well as claiming an exemption for foreign sourced income.

There is also no capital gains tax in Labuan.

In addition to this, Labuan does not impose any disclosure requirements as regards beneficial ownership. It has, however, committed to the OECD's tax standard on the exchange of information and is now on the OECD 'white list'.

So, all in all, it offers some attractive tax-saving opportunities, depending on your own personal residence position, plus some attractive privacy protection benefits. Labuan has also announced that it is undertaking a review of its offshore laws to make it even more attractive.

FLOATING TAX HAVENS

If you like travelling and are fond of the sea you could consider living on a boat. You would need to be careful about where you locate it as it wouldn't be possible to simply moor offshore and claim non-residence status.

Most developed countries also tax individuals living on boats within their territorial waters. The UK, for example, taxes individuals within 12 nautical miles of the shore.

Alternatively, if you have a few million to spare and are a member of the super-rich you could buy an apartment on *The World*, which is a newly launched luxury cruise ship (you can visit www.aboardtheworld.com for more information).

Getting yourself an apartment on this luxury super ship doesn't come cheap. About 110 permanent apartments with between one and three bedrooms were for sale on the ship with prices starting at £1.6 million and rising to over £5 million.

This amount of money buys you a luxurious fully fitted apartment (with internet access, of course, so you can do business while cruising around the globe!).

The key benefit of *The World* is that the ship sails around the world all year round so people who live on board can be true 'nautical nomads' and escape being classed as tax resident in any particular country (although US citizens would need to be careful, as a tax charge could apply even if non-resident).

Whilst this is certainly beneficial you should note that if you are conducting a trade in a particular country, you could still have to pay tax in the country where the business is based, unless, of course, you are trading out of a tax haven. Furthermore, you would not be able to make use of any double tax treaties (as you wouldn't be officially resident anywhere!) to reduce any withholding taxes that you may be subject to.

If you want to go one step further you could consider joining one of the 'offshore communities' being proposed. The plan is to create an entire town in the middle of the sea (on a mobile platform). There will be houses, shops, recreation facilities etc. and the platform will travel the globe, remaining in international waters.

Whether many people could live so cut off from the rest of the world is debatable. However, it would be the ultimate tax haven with no taxes at all. One point to bear in mind is that you'd also need to carefully consider whether your home country would accept that you are non-resident if you cannot prove that you are resident in another country.

Another alternative is to purchase your own yacht.

When most people think of yachts they think of the impressive boats you find moored in jet-set locations such as Monaco. However, if sailing is your thing, you could probably purchase a large yacht capable of comfortable and safe ocean travel for under $200,000.

It would be kitted out like a home from home and most would offer air-conditioning and all the latest mod cons.

Again you would need to travel pretty regularly in order to avoid being classed as resident in any jurisdiction, however this may not be that difficult in practice.

It's likely that the number of 'nautical nomads' will continue to grow in places where countries are close and welcome visitors. The Caribbean is a perfect example as some of the islands are within 25 miles of each other and many permit visitors to stay for three months at a time on tourists visas.

What's more, many of the Caribbean countries have no taxes, so even if you do stay for too long in any one jurisdiction, the tax implications may not be significant.

CHAPTER 3

LIVING IN A TAX HAVEN

Possibly the easiest way to escape tax in one country is to move to another!

With more and more people 'telecommuting' (working from remote mobile offices), doing your job or running your business in another country may not prove such a problem.

While most countries, such as the UK, tax the worldwide income of their residents, they do not tax citizens who leave the country and become non-resident.

So a UK a citizen can escape high UK tax bills simply by moving to a low-tax country.

Most countries treat you as non-resident if you are absent for six to nine months.

However this is not always the case. The US, for example, taxes its *citizens*, no matter where they live.

So if you're a US citizen and go and live in the Bahamas for 10 years you'll still have to pay US tax on all your income (subject to a limited exemption for overseas earned income).

To escape the US tax net completely you would have to relinquish your citizenship and acquire another one.

Citizens of most other countries, such as the UK, can escape the taxman's clutches by becoming non-resident.

However, certain countries make it more difficult than others to lose your resident status.

For example, in Sweden you are regarded as resident if:

- Your 'real home and dwelling' is in Sweden, or
- Your 'habitual abode' is in Sweden, or

- You previously had a 'real home and dwelling' there and you have an 'essential connection' with Sweden.

'Essential connection' means, for instance, that you had Swedish property or family in Sweden.

Another big stumbling block is that anyone who has spent more then 10 years in Sweden is deemed to remain resident for five years after leaving, unless they can prove that they have no 'essential connection' with the country.

Similar rules apply in Holland. The factors that determine your residence status include the number of days you spend in Holland during the tax year, whether you own Dutch property and whether you have any family there.

This shows how easy it is to come within the scope of two countries' tax regimes. A Swedish person emigrating to the US could easily be classed as both Swedish resident, as well as US resident (if they actually live in the US). In this case, though, the US-Sweden tax treaty would come into play to decide in which of the two countries the individual is resident.

The Dutch sometimes also levy an 'exit' tax on residents and inheritance tax applies for up to 10 years after your residence has ceased. So avoiding Dutch tax is a long-term process.

However, the EU Commission has been looking at a number of 'exit taxes' in France, Germany and the Netherlands on the grounds that they prevent free movement of people within the EU. In March 2010 the EU requested some countries such as Belgium and Denmark remove the exit tax regime for companies and has referred some countries to the EU Court of Justice.

Following a ruling by the European Court of Justice the Dutch exit tax regime has been changed. Tax can be deferred until capital gains are actually realized. The US has also implemented an exit tax regime for some individuals who want to give up their citizenship.

Other countries also have an 'emigration tax'.

For example, let's say you have UK investment property and become Australian resident. When you eventually sell the property you will only pay Australian capital gains tax on profits made *after* entering the country. All your profits made prior to becoming an Australian resident will be tax free.

In tax speak we say there is an 'uplift' in the asset's base cost: the cost of the asset is no longer what you paid for it but is deemed to be its market value when you entered the country. A higher cost means less profit and therefore less tax.

The drawback is that if you cease to be Australian resident your investments are deemed to have been sold (even if they haven't) which means that emigrants can end up with hefty capital gains tax bills when they leave the country.

There is fortunately a concession (known as the '5-in-10' concession) which exempts assets held by anyone who has lived in Australia for less than five out of the previous 10 years. As a result many expat workers are not trapped by this piece of tax law.

In summary, moving overseas can be an effective way to drastically cut your tax bill. Some countries like the UK will largely stop taxing you when you leave while others, like the US, will tax you wherever you go.

The Source Basis vs The Residence Basis

It's important to distinguish between the 'source' basis of taxation and the 'residence' basis. Most countries use one or the other.

Under the source basis it doesn't matter what your residence status is: your income is taxed if it arises within the country's borders. So if you are a resident of Atlantis and emigrate to Narnia, you will still have to pay tax in Atlantis on the investments you left behind. By contrast, under the residence basis, Atlantis will stop taxing you once you become non-resident.

A lot of countries tax income that arises within their borders by default. For example, tax is deducted in the UK from interest earned by non-residents however, they can apply to have interest paid gross (without tax deducted).

You have to be careful if you plan to move to a tax haven and continue running a business in your home country. Most countries tax trading income arising within their boundaries.

There are, however, two exceptions to this rule:

- If you go and live in a country that has a double tax treaty with the country where your business is based. In this case you will probably only pay local tax on profits arising from a permanent establishment (in other words, a business with a physical presence in the country, such as offices).

- The problem is finding a country that has a good double tax treaty network AND a low domestic tax regime. This is why Cyprus and Ireland are popular tax havens.

- If your business is based in a genuine 'no tax' haven. There would then be no local taxes on your trading profits.

Becoming a UK Non-Resident

In the March 2011 Budget it was announced that HMRC would be bringing in a new statutory residence test ("SRT"). This applies from April 2013.

The new test brings a range of "key" factors into account when assessing residence. Rather than considering a lot of vague and uncertain factors, you can determine your residence by looking at the factors laid out in the legislation.

Legislation focuses on the key UK ties such as having UK accommodation, UK family or UK employment. Other less important ties such as UK clubs, UK burial plot ownership, and UK bank accounts are not included in the new test.

Therefore in most cases you will only need to consider the specific factors laid out in the legislation.

There is still the odd subjective element to the new rules. For instance having a UK home will make you automatically UK resident in many cases. However "home" isn't accurately defined and you need to look at whether, on the facts, a UK property is your home.

There is also a system of recognising that to establish non residence, there can be more ties with the UK if there are fewer visits. They use a scale which takes account of different UK ties according to the length of UK visits and whether you are a "leaver" or an "arriver".

The Government was clear on this and they said that to avoid the complexity of previous case law:

- the test should not take into account a wide range of connections;

- relevant connections should be simply and clearly defined;
- the weight and relevance of each connection should be clear.

The test has been designed so that it is harder to become non-resident when leaving the UK after a period of residence than it is to become resident when an individual comes to the UK.

Once an individual has become resident and built up connections with the UK, they should be required to scale back their ties to the UK significantly, spend far less time here, or a combination of the two before they can relinquish residence.

This is consistent with the principle, reflected in case law, that residence should have an adhesive nature.

Capital Gains Tax Planning

One of the main reasons people use tax havens is to escape capital gains tax (CGT). Individuals with large property or share portfolios or a business to sell often consider moving overseas to a country with low or no capital gains tax. To do this successfully UK residents must ensure they are not UK resident or UK ordinarily resident. The good news is that, if CGT avoidance is your top priority, there are a lot of countries that don't tax capital gains.

Cyprus is a popular choice for UK expats because it allows you to avoid CGT on UK land and property disposals and also offers advantageous income tax treatment of pensions.

The Chancellor announced in his 2013 Autumn Statement that he will consult during 2014 on a proposed capital gains tax for non resident investors in UK residential property.

The tax is intended to have effect from April 2015. This is a further extension of the scope of UK tax - and is intended to be in addition to the CGT regime for 'enveloped' dwellings within "Annual Tax On Enveloped Dwellings" (ATED) which came in during 2013.

Unlike that regime, it seems the new tax will apply to residential property let to third parties so is firmly intended to tax investment gains

The Importance of Timing

Timing is crucial in offshore tax planning and should be built into your 'escape plan' from early on.

For example, there's no point moving to a tax haven to sell your investment properties if you still end up paying tax in the country you leave.

This could easily happen if you don't understand your home country's capital gains tax rules for emigrants. For example, it could be the case that you can become non-resident half way through a tax year for *income tax* purposes. But for *capital gains tax* purposes you may need to be a non-resident for the entire tax year.

If you leave the UK and sell assets later in *the same tax year*, you will still have to pay UK capital gains tax unless you qualify for the split year basis.

To avoid capital gains tax you have to sell your assets in the *next tax year*.

You'll also find similar rules in the US, as well as many other European countries.

Another way you may get caught out is by selling assets en route to another high-tax country. For example, if you emigrate from the UK to Country X and decide to stop off in the Cayman Islands to dispose of your UK properties, any gain could still be subject to tax in Country X if you're classed as resident for that tax year.

Therefore as a general rule you are much safer if you conduct all your dealings in *separate tax years*:

- Dispose of assets in a separate tax year from the year you emigrate.
- Dispose of assets, if possible, in a separate tax year from the year you acquire residence in your new home country.

Clearly it is crucial to understand how different countries apply the definition of residence.

If you can find a country that allows 'split-year' residence you may have nothing to fear. The split-year basis means that you will only pay tax on income or gains that arise *after* you become a resident in that country.

So if you sell assets early in the tax year and then become resident in another country a few months later, you won't be taxed.

The UK applies such a split-year rule in certain circumstances, as does the US.

You become a US resident for tax purposes as soon as you become a permanent resident. You will then have to declare your worldwide income to the IRS.

Of course lots of immigrants find themselves becoming US resident during a tax year, with part of the tax year having been spent in another country such as the UK.

This is known as a 'dual status' tax year. As a dual-status taxpayer you will be taxed on income and capital gains from all sources for the part of the year you are a US resident.

You will also be taxed on income and gains derived in the US for the entire tax year. Income from a trade or business conducted in the United States will also be taxed.

Note that income and gains you receive from sources outside the US before you become resident is usually not taxable. Therefore if you acquire US residence via a green card you can usually escape US tax by selling any overseas assets prior to actually becoming US resident.

Some people become 'tax nomads' ensuring they are not resident in any country. This is difficult to achieve long term but ideal for a couple of years to shield large capital gains or one-off income payments.

However, if you keep hold of income-producing assets in your home country your options are more limited. UK rental income and trading income, for example, is usually taxed even if you become non-resident.

Most tax treaties between countries state that the country where the property is physically located can tax the rental income. In the UK the Non-resident Landlord Scheme requires letting agent or tenants to withhold tax from the rent paid to an overseas landlord.

In these cases the main focus is on maximizing your tax deductions.

Ways you could do this include moving offshore and forming an offshore personal service company that invoices your UK trading company. These amounts would be tax deductible and reduce your taxable profits in the UK. At the same time the payments from the UK company could be received tax free.

As for rental income, obtaining offshore loans and claiming the interest as a tax deduction is a popular technique.

CHAPTER 4

HOW OFFSHORE TRUSTS CAN HELP YOU

What is a Trust?

Offshore trusts are set up for lots of different reasons. The most popular are tax avoidance and privacy protection. For example, offshore trusts are often used in conjunction with offshore companies. By making a trust a shareholder of the company the beneficial ownership of the company can stay completely confidential.

The beauty of a trust is that it lets you transfer ownership of your assets while still having a say as to how they are used. So rather than give a large cash amount to your teenage son, you could establish a trust for his benefit, and transfer the cash to the trust. As well as having important family financial planning benefits, they can also have tax and asset protection advantages.

The basic idea is that if the assets are no longer yours you don't have to pay tax. And if the assets aren't legally yours, creditors and others won't be able to get their hands on them either.

There are various people involved in setting up and running a trust:

•   **Trustees**. These are the people who actually run the trust and decide how the trust's assets are used (subject to the trust agreement). There are usually at least two trustees and, as their name implies, it's essential that they are people you can trust.

•   In some cases a professional trustee may be used. This could be either a solicitor, accountant or a firm that specializes in trust administration. There are lots of specialist trust firms based in the various tax havens.

•   **Beneficiaries**. These are the individuals who actually benefit from the trust's assets. They could, for example, be allowed to use a property owned by the trust or receive income from the trust's investments.

•   Beneficiaries can have different types of interest in the assets. For example, a life interest could allow a property to be used during a beneficiary's lifetime. A residual interest would then give someone else the right to benefit after the life interest beneficiary has died.

- **Settlor**. The settlor is the individual who gifts the assets to the trust in the first place. Unless the settlor is also a trustee he will have no automatic influence over how the assets are used, although as a matter of course the trustees would be guided by the settlor, especially if he has chosen them well.

Apart from choosing the trustees carefully, there are three key ways that a settlor can provide guidance as to how the trust assets are used:

- First, the settlor can draft a letter of wishes. The content of the letter will be entirely up to the particular settlor. It could be a general letter covering his aims in setting up the trust and what he hopes to achieve or it could be a highly specific letter listing allowable and non allowable payments from the trust.

- Typically, the letter of wishes will show the trustees what the settlor's purpose was in setting up the trust, the type of investments the trust should make and the type of payouts the trustees should consider. Although not binding, the letter of wishes would usually be taken seriously by the trustees.

- Second, and perhaps most important, is the trust agreement. This is the document that actually establishes the trust and will provide the scope of the trustees powers. The settlor should ensure that any particular requirements regarding the trust are set out clearly in this document.

- One of the most important functions of the trust agreement is defining when and under what circumstances the beneficiaries will be entitled to benefit from the trust.

- Thirdly, the settlor could set himself up as a 'protector' of the trust.

A protector is a special category completely separate from the trustees and beneficiaries. They usually have the power to add or remove trustees. This provides additional certainty that trustees will give due consideration to the settlor's wishes.

There is a high degree of flexibility particularly as to the terms of the trust agreement. This could lay out various conditions that have to be met before benefits can be enjoyed.

Typical conditions could be:

- Preventing minors from benefiting until they reach a certain age, for example 18 or 21.
- Stopping trust benefits once beneficiaries exceed a certain age, for example 30.
- Providing benefits to future grandchildren.
- Ceasing benefits if beneficiaries become non-resident.
- Granting benefits as reward for specific achievements such as obtaining a university degree or other qualification.
- Stopping trust benefits when a beneficiary becomes married or remarries.

Tax Benefits of Trusts

Trusts can be used for a variety of tax-saving purposes. One of the most popular is emigration tax planning.

Someone who has decided to emigrate could transfer a substantial part of their assets to an offshore trust before taking up residence in the new country. The idea here is to prevent the new country taxing the immigrant's income and assets.

A good example of how trusts can be used is for UK immigrants.

UK Immigrants

Trusts are also used by those who emigrate to the UK. Assets could be transferred into an offshore trust prior to obtaining UK residence. The assets of the offshore trust would then not be part of the immigrant's estate for inheritance tax purposes.

Similar principles apply in other countries and if your intention is to own assets in a high-tax country, using an offshore trust will often take the assets out of the scope of certain domestic taxes. Inheritance taxes, in particular, can be avoided by setting up offshore trusts.

UK Residents and Trusts

There are a number of provisions designed to prevent people who already live in the UK setting up an offshore trust and escaping the taxman's clutches.

These 'trust-busting' rules are highly complex but the basic gist in that they can be used to force the person who sets up the trust or the beneficiaries to pay tax on the trust's income and capital gains.

Anyone wanting to set up a trust should always take professional advice to find out whether these trust-busting rules will apply.

The following are some of the situations where an offshore trust could still be used effectively by a UK resident:

Where the *Settlor* Is Not UK Domiciled

People who are not UK domiciled are in a privileged position as they can potentially use trusts to avoid certain UK taxes.

For example, a non-domiciled person could establish a trust to hold overseas property. If the trust is classed as an 'excluded property trust' the assets would fall out of the UK inheritance tax net.

Those who intend to live in the UK for the long term (but are not UK domiciled) could use this arrangement to protect their overseas assets in the event that they become UK domiciled (you can be deemed UK domiciled for inheritance tax purposes after having been resident for 17 years).

Where the *Beneficiaries* Are Not UK Domiciled

Anti-avoidance rules tax capital gains in the hands of a trust's beneficiaries in certain circumstances. However, if the beneficiaries are non-UK domiciled (or non-UK resident) these rules may not apply, and if they do would probably only apply where beneficiaries remit gains to the UK so long as they are subject to the remittance basis of tax. An offshore trust could therefore realize gains and make overseas payments to UK resident but non-domiciled individuals free of tax.

Where No Family Members Are Beneficiaries

These are difficult to achieve in practice but could be made by remote relations or friends. These offshore trusts would act as a shelter from UK tax on both income and capital gains. This means that any gains or overseas income the trust generates would not be taxed in the hands of the settlor.

Where the Trust Is for Income Tax Avoidance & the Beneficiaries are Grandchildren

The capital gains tax anti-avoidance provisions are much stricter than the income tax provisions. Therefore while an offshore trust formed with grandchildren being the beneficiaries would be exempt from UK income tax on overseas income and gains, the gains of the trust would be attributed to a UK-resident settlor of the trust. The overseas income would not, however, so the trust could avoid paying any UK tax on any foreign income.

Where the Trust Owns Shares in Overseas Trading Companies

There are a couple of reasons why using a trust to own shares in overseas trading companies may prove effective. Firstly, a UK resident would find it easier to argue that a company is non-UK resident if the shares are owned by a non-UK resident trust.

Secondly, and linked to trusts for grandchildren, a common example would be for the trust to hold shares in a non-UK resident trading company (operating wholly abroad). Profits would be paid to the trust from the company but as this represents foreign income it would not be apportioned to the UK resident taxpayer and could be held in the trust to benefit the grandchildren.

One of the main problems for a UK resident thinking of setting up an offshore trust is that any capital gains from property, shares and other assets could be taxed if the settlor or his family can benefit from the trust.

Similarly, income of the trust could be taxed if the settlor, his spouse or minor children can benefit.

Therefore simply setting up a trust to hold overseas assets for the benefit of a settlor and his spouse is unlikely to yield any UK tax advantages.

As for inheritance tax, establishing a trust can be beneficial as it can take the assets out of the estate of the transferor. However, in the UK most trusts are subject to a separate inheritance tax regime, so avoiding inheritance tax by using trusts is certainly not straightforward, although it's fair to say that they can be used to reduce tax.

Offshore Companies Owned by a Trust

Offshore trusts are often used together with offshore companies for enhanced confidentiality.

There are different types of trusts, however you would usually use a discretionary trust for this type of arrangement. With a discretionary trust the trustees are able to use their 'discretion' as to who benefits and by how much.

Often such trusts are formed to guarantee privacy over your assets. You may not need to be a named beneficiary of this type of trust – or named in any other way.

To make this work, the trustee and the settlor would usually all be residents of a country other than your own.

The discretionary trust would then own the offshore company which itself would own various assets such as property.

The offshore company can have a nominee director and secretary or alternatively you could use bearer shares if you use an International Business Company (IBC) incorporated in a suitable jurisdiction (for example, a Cayman exempt company).

With bearer shares the person who holds the share certificates is the person who owns the company. Ownership is transferred simply by handing over the share certificates to someone else.

They're available in a number of offshore tax havens specializing in privacy protection. In many jurisdictions, using an offshore trust and company structure would allow you to legally absolve yourself of ownership of the offshore company and its assets, which would instead be owned by the trust.

For UK individuals, using the offshore trust/company structure is often beneficial as it would make it easier to argue that the company itself is not UK resident.

An offshore company could still be UK resident (and therefore subject to

UK taxes on worldwide income and gains) if it is controlled and managed from the UK.

If there are UK directors and shareholders it would be difficult to argue that the company is not managed and controlled from the UK.

By using an offshore trust to hold the shares in the company, provided it is the offshore trustees that exercise control over the directors, it is easier to argue the company is controlled outside the UK and is non-resident (resulting in overseas income and capital gains being exempt from UK corporation tax).

Another common scenario is for the settlor (the person who sets up the trust) to offer services to the trust for a fee (for example, managing properties or investigating investment opportunities).

In this role, you can also claim expenses for costs you incur as well as take out a loan from the company and purchase assets for the company.

Note that you'd need to be careful to ensure that legal documentation was in place to clearly establish the relationship between you and the offshore company.

This allows you to extract cash from the trust without remaining a trust beneficiary. This can be useful because, as we've seen, many jurisdictions, such as the UK and many European countries, have anti-avoidance legislation that applies where a settlor is also a beneficiary.

These rules can force the settlor to pay tax on the income of the trust. Using the independent contractor route can help to circumvent these rules.

If you're looking at establishing a trust, as stated previously, you should ensure that you have trustees that you really can trust. It's also advisable to have a trust 'protector' who can replace the trustees if necessary.

The cost of setting up an offshore trust structure will vary depending on the type of trust and whether there are any offshore companies involved.

You're probably looking at less than £1,000 for a simple trust to over £10,000 for a more complex arrangement.

Where Is the Best Place to Locate an Offshore Trust?

There are numerous countries that offer a good regime for setting up an offshore trust.

A trust can operate anywhere in the world. The only requirement is that the jurisdiction under which the trust is established recognizes the legal concept of the trust.

Aside from the tax implications you should consider the running of the trust and keep an eye of the costs involved (both the initial set up costs and the ongoing administration costs).

For most people the most important considerations when deciding where to set up an offshore trust are:

- Asset protection and confidentiality
- Tax savings

The countries below are all recognized as good places to set up an offshore trust:

- Jersey/Guernsey
- Liechtenstein
- St Kitts and Nevis
- Panama
- The Bahamas
- Austria
- New Zealand
- Netherlands Antilles

This list is by no means exhaustive and depending on the use of the trust and location of the beneficiaries and settlor, other countries such as Mauritius and Belize could also be considered.

In particular, significant non-tax considerations could be paramount including:

- The language used in the jurisdiction
- The time difference between you and the country in question
- The political and financial stability of the tax haven
- The geographical location – in case you need to visit in person
- The costs associated with setting up and running the trust

For example, someone wanting to trade with China might be better off setting up a trust in Mauritius as opposed to St Kitts, due to Mauritius's proximity and good relationship with China.

CHAPTER 5

ESCAPING THE TAXMAN'S CLUTCHES

Many high-tax countries have what are known as 'controlled foreign company' (CFC) laws to prevent people making use of tax havens.

Essentially the fact that the company is located in a tax haven is ignored and the profits are all taxed in, say, the UK if the company is viewed as being controlled by someone living in the UK.

These laws are designed to stop individuals and companies shifting profits to tax havens.

The exact arrangements vary widely from country to country but countries that have CFC rules include:

- United States
- United Kingdom
- Canada
- Australia
- Spain
- France
- Germany

So if you're considering using an offshore company or trust you should always look at the CFC or other anti-avoidance rules in your country of residence and assess how they affect your tax planning.

You can then look at the options available for circumventing these rules. A common example is to ensure that you don't fall foul of the 'ownership requirement'.

Many CFC regulations impose a minimum ownership of the overseas entity before the rules will 'bite'. Provided you own less than the minimum you should be safe. For instance, the UK has special controlled foreign company legislation that affects any overseas company that is owned by a UK company.

If the overseas company is classed as a CFC, its profits are apportioned to any UK companies who hold an interest in it, provided the percentage of the profits apportioned is at least 25%.

There are however some exemptions available to prevent the CFC rules from applying.

Before falling within the CFC rules a company would first need to meet the definition of a 'controlled foreign company'.

A CFC is defined as a *company* that is:

- Not UK resident,
- Controlled from the UK, and
- Subject to overseas tax which is less than 75% of the equivalent UK tax.

So the first point to note is that the UK CFC regime will not apply if you are an individual owning an overseas company. (Instead other anti-avoidance legislation could apply which we'll look at shortly.)

Therefore the CFC provisions are going to apply to overseas companies established in low tax countries. What you would need to do is calculate the company's profits and find out what the overseas tax charge is. You then calculate the UK tax liability and if the overseas tax paid is less than three-quarters of the UK tax, the overseas company could fall within the CFC provisions.

There is a new regime applying from 2012 and the big news for SMEs is that the de-minimis profits limit will be raised from £50,000 per annum to £500,000 per annum, an increase of tenfold. Most SMEs will therefore fall outside the scope of the CFC rules.

The US by contrast has its own CFC legislation. It defines a CFC as:

"any foreign corporation of which more than fifty percent of its value or voting stock is owned by United States shareholders on any one day during the taxable year of such Foreign Corporation".

A US shareholder is also specifically defined as a US citizen or entity (in other words, an individual or a company or trust) holding or controlling more than 10% of the shares.

Example

Let's say that the shares in Bob Ltd, a British Virgin Islands company, are held by the following people:
- *Jake a US resident owns 50%*
- *Jason a US resident owns 11%*
- *Peter a resident of the Caymans owns 39%*

Under the existing US tax rules, Bob Inc is a CFC because more than 50% of the voting stock is held by US shareholders. As a result, the profits of the CFC could be apportioned directly to the shareholders and taxed in the US.

The simplest way to avoid ending up with a CFC is to ensure that less than 50% of the shares are held by US shareholders – and no individual shareholder holds more than 10% of the shares. One way of doing this is to use a foundation or trust to hold more than 50% of the shares.

However, in the US there are also passive investment rules that could apply.

The US tax authorities make a distinction between income earned from a foreign business and income generated by passive investments. Income earned by a trading business can usually stay untaxed until it is extracted by a US resident. Investment income usually becomes caught up in the passive investment rules that result in a much more complicated and unfavourable tax treatment and can lead to unrealised profits being taxed.

Examples of How to Commonly Avoid the CFC Rules

- Set up a new business in a tax haven such as Cyprus or Gibraltar with ownership that falls outside the CFC rules (for example, for US tax purposes don't hold more than 40% from US shareholders) and put the rest of the shares in trust for children or in the hands of an offshore relative.

- Create a joint venture with other companies or individuals so that ownership is sufficiently diversified so that you escape the CFC rules and the ownership requirements.

UK Provisions for Individuals

You'll notice from this that the US provisions apply to individuals and companies, whereas the UK provisions only apply to companies. This doesn't mean that UK individuals have free rein to use offshore companies and trusts.

The UK has similar provisions that apply to individuals in the Income Tax Act 2007. One of these is S720. This gives the taxman wide-ranging powers to prevent income tax avoidance by individuals using offshore companies and trusts.

S720 applies to an individual who transfers assets or is associated with a transfer by somebody else. The conditions for application of Section 720 are broadly:

- There must be a transfer of assets by an individual.
- As a result of the transfer, income becomes payable to a non-resident person.
- The transferor must have power to enjoy the income.
- The transferor must be UK resident during the year in question.

If all of these conditions are fulfilled the income that becomes payable to the offshore company or trust is deemed to be that of the individual who made the transfer, to the extent that he has power to enjoy that income.

The first point to consider is whether there has been a 'transfer of assets' by you. The UK tax authorities take a wide view of what constitutes a transfer of assets. For example, S720 may apply where an individual transfers cash to establish a non-resident trust or subscribes for the share capital of an offshore company or where an individual transfers assets such as shares or property to a new or existing non-resident company or trust in a tax haven.

It can also apply where intangible assets are transferred, for example where a UK individual transfers his services to an offshore company.

If the conditions above are satisfied, the income of the non-resident company or trust can be taxed under S720, whether it's UK source income or foreign source income.

Note that one of the above conditions is that the UK resident must have power to enjoy the income of the overseas vehicle (for example, as a shareholder of an overseas company or as a beneficiary of a non-resident trust).

Even if you did not actually receive any income from the trust it is the *potential* to enjoy the income that matters. As such you would not have to actually receive any of the income at all.

Another provision Revenue and Customs could use is S731. This applies where assets have been transferred abroad and a UK resident other than the settlor obtains a benefit. The beneficiaries then have to pay tax. For this rule to apply the following conditions must be satisfied:

- There must be a transfer of assets.
- As a result of the transfer, income becomes payable to a non-resident person.
- As a result of the transfer, an individual other than the transferor receives a benefit, which isn't otherwise taxed.
- The person who receives the benefit must be resident in the UK.

Section 731 is different from Section 720 in that it taxes *non-transferors* on the benefits they receive.

Benefits which are taxed in terms of Section 731 include payments of any kind, for example cash (capital distributions), the use of property (such as occupation of a house) and interest-free loans. Where the conditions are satisfied, the individual receiving the benefit is liable to pay tax on the amount or value of the benefit.

It's worth noting that S720 and S731 apply unless you can show that an exemption applies. You would need to show that:

- Tax avoidance was not the purpose or one of the purposes for which the transfer took place, or

- The transfer and any associated operations were genuine commercial transactions AND were not designed for the purpose of avoiding tax.

Actually persuading the taxman that you can take advantage of this exemption can in practice be difficult. There are typically two circumstances in which it is applied:

- Firstly, where the purpose of the transaction was the avoidance of *overseas* tax (as opposed to UK tax).

- Secondly, where the settlor and his spouse are wholly excluded from the settlement. If you were excluded from benefiting from the trust, this would make it much clearer that the purpose of the offshore settlement was not tax driven, given that you would suffer the real economic consequence of losing all possibility of benefiting from your assets.

So there you have it. The CFC rules in whatever guise need to be carefully looked into when considering any form of overseas company or trust.

Use of Foundations

Foundations have become increasingly popular in recent years and offer some of the advantages of trusts while avoiding many of the pitfalls.

Residents of many English-speaking countries view offshore trusts with a certain amount of suspicion. The tax authorities are the most cynical of all and have introduced various pieces of trust-busting legislation over the years.

This has increased the appeal of alternative structures, such as the Private Interest Foundation (PIF).

What is a Foundation?

Foundations are similar to trusts in many ways although there are some crucial differences.

Just like setting up a trust, when an individual sets up a foundation they transfer control over their assets to another person. In other words, the foundation is a separate entity to the settlor.

When a settlor transfers assets to a trust, the trustees hold the assets on behalf of the trust beneficiaries. The trustees are also bound by the trust agreement. However, with a foundation, the foundation itself has a separate legal personality.

As a result the foundation can enter into agreements as it is the owner of the assets which are managed by the foundation council.

By contrast a trust is not a separate legal entity different from the trustee (although it is separate from the settlor).

How You Can Use a Foundation

One of the most popular uses for foundations is to hold shares in an international business company (IBC). This puts ownership of the IBC in the hands of a separate legal entity and away from the actual beneficial owner.

Much is made of the benefits that a foundation structure can provide, but essentially the main reason to do this is to demonstrate that the IBC is not controlled by you from your country of residence. Whether this is successful or not in tax terms will likely depend on the anti avoidance rules in your country of residence. In the UK for instance, the foundation is treated for tax purposes in a similar way to a company. This is not to say that a foundation would not be beneficial for UK residents/domiciliaries, as it could still be a valuable asset protection tool.

If you could navigate the anti-avoidance rules you may then prevent the IBC from being classed as resident in your home country. In the case of the UK this could ensure that the IBC's overseas income and gains are not subject to UK tax.

Most people would use a professional firm to manage and set up such a structure. It makes sense to ensure that the management team are resident in a country other than your own and preferably in a country which has strict privacy laws (such as Liechtenstein or Panama).

A foundation can therefore exist simply as an intermediary, with its main purpose being to take ownership of the company out of your hands so that you are not subject to your country's reporting and tax requirements.

Note that if you are a beneficiary of the foundation, this could then bring you within many countries' anti-avoidance 'trust-busting' rules, with the result that you end up being taxed. Therefore to keep the benefits you should conduct the business of the corporation 'at arm's length'.

In practical terms all day-to-day transactions should be carried out by the IBC on an arm's length basis. For maximum safety you could also consider appointing a professional management firm to be the signatory to the IBC bank account.

Mention this to most people and you can expect a healthy degree of scepticism. After all there's a risk they could take your hard-earned cash and do a moonlight flit.

In reality, provided you use a reputable firm as signatory, this is highly unlikely. Many of the offshore jurisdictions where such firms are located rely on the offshore industry for a lot of their revenues (company registration fees and other taxes). As a result tax haven Governments are keen to protect the reputation of their offshore sectors as much as possible. Strict business confidentiality laws also usually accompany the low taxes.

You should also bear in mind the OECD's exchange of information rules, although these will not be a significant issue if you fully disclose to the tax authority in your home country (where necessary).

Many law firms will offer signatory services and this could offer double protection as obtaining such services from a reputable law firm would make it unlikely that a breach of trust would occur. The annual charges for an external signatory range from £500 to £1,500 and therefore whether this is worthwhile may depend on the usage of the account and the value of funds in it.

The benefit of this arrangement is that you enjoy maximum protection and it would be difficult to argue that you control the IBC or foundation, particularly if you also use nominee directors and nominee foundation members. You would be behind the scenes only and would not own or 'control' the assets. Note that although the nominees would control the IBC, you could usually make recommendations to them.

You would, of course, need to set up such a structure after carefully reviewing the tax rules in your home country.

If you are the signatory on an offshore account, many countries such as the US impose some hefty fines for failure to report this.

Another perceived advantage of the foundation and IBC structure is that it can allow traders to avoid paying any tax until they withdraw income or capital gains out of the foundation. The reasoning behind this is that many countries look to whether an offshore corporation is controlled by a resident when deciding if the corporation itself is resident and therefore subject to tax in the home country.

If that taxpayer does not have legal ownership in the company (because the foundation does), many countries' tax rules state that no tax is payable on profits of the company that are not extracted, although obviously they would tax any receipts that came from the company.

There are two caveats here. Firstly, you would need to look at your home country's CFC rules to see if the IBC falls within their scope. If it does, the fact that the profits are not extracted would be irrelevant and they could be taxed in your hands.

Secondly, US citizens have specific rules relating to investment income in such circumstances. If a proportion of the income earned by the IBC is derived from passive investment income, the IRS would take the view that the income would be taxable when earned as opposed to when it's brought back into the country.

This is a pretty unusual view and most countries do not take this stance.

Getting Your Money into the Company

If you're looking to invest some large funds into the IBC/foundation you have to be careful about falling foul of rules relating to gifts in your home country. For example, the UK, US and many European countries operate gift taxes that could tax a simple transfer of cash or assets (either under inheritance tax or capital gains tax laws).

However, if you obtain something of equal value in return for the transfer there cannot be said to be a 'gift'. So a transfer in exchange for share capital should not be a gift and could allow the company to be capitalised with minimal tax costs.

In terms of extracting cash one option for getting cash out of the offshore company could be in the form of a loan from the IBC.

In order to keep to the arm's length principle, the loan could be structured in the form of a 'balloon note', which would roll up interest and become payable in a number of years.

Some balloon notes are for 20-year terms and are then renegotiated when the maturity date arrives.

In terms of most offshore IBCs there would be no problem with this.

What you would need to look at is whether your home country has any anti-avoidance rules that could effectively tax the loan repayment or, more accurately, the interest element.

Aside from the tax benefits of using the foundation, there are also non-tax benefits including:

- **Privacy.** The privacy benefits are substantial and are one of the key reasons for using the foundation structure. The foundation offers strict confidentiality as regards ownership. Your privacy is easier to protect as you are not usually a beneficiary in any way and would not have any beneficial interest in the foundation assets.

- **Excellent Asset Protection.** Foundations are increasingly used by professionals in high-risk sectors, such as doctors, lawyers, consultants, dentists and accountants, many of whom are at risk of potentially huge liability claims, to protect their assets from creditors.

The key issue here is beneficial ownership. If you own the assets, they would usually be classed as part of your estate and would be available to potential creditors.

However, with a foundation you are no longer the owner of either the beneficial or legal interest in the foundation assets.

This would make it much more difficult for the courts or anyone else to prove that you retained beneficial ownership as the foundation exists completely separately and independently from you and is a separate entity.

It has its own governing council members who direct how the foundation assets will be used.

The IBC/foundation package can also be used for enhanced 'bullet-proof' property protection against creditors.

For example, using a simple company structure an IBC or limited liability company (LLC) could hold the title to some land.

A mortgage can be placed on the property by the company, thus absorbing any equity in it. This would make it less attractive to creditors in the case of a lawsuit or dispute.

To make this 'bullet-proof' you could also use a foundation. If it was a US based individual for instance, a Delaware or Nevada LLC would own the land, which would in turn be owned by a separate PIF for asset protection purposes.

When to Use a Foundation

Some of the most common scenarios are:

- Estate planning to pass assets on to children/grandchildren
- To provide for children or other family members
- To protect assets against potential creditors
- To collect royalties
- To invest in the stock market
- As a property investment vehicle
- To operate bank accounts

Best Places to Set Up a Foundation

Not all countries permit a foundation structure. The UK and US for example do not contain foundation provisions within their legislation.

There are a variety of countries that offer a foundation including:

- Liechtenstein
- Panama
- Canada
- Luxembourg
- Austria

The most popular locations are Panama and Liechtenstein which get most of the foundation business. The main reason for this is that these are to some extent 'general purpose' foundations that can offer advantages in other jurisdictions as well. By contrast countries such as Canada offer foundations that are particularly suited to Canadian residents.

What to Look for in a Good Foundation

- **Privacy and anonymity**. Panama and Liechtenstein are good choices as they traditionally required that the foundation maintained strict secrecy, although this has been watered down somewhat by the exchange of information provisions with overseas authorities.

- **No taxes.** Both Panama and Liechtenstein can provide zero tax foundations.

- **Limited regulation**. You'll probably want to do away with an annual general meeting and the requirement to file annual returns.

- **Cost**. Some jurisdictions have relatively cheap fees with incorporation possible for less than $1,500.

- **Flexibility**. For many it's essential not to be tied to the country where the foundation is established (eg Panama or Liechtenstein).

In essence, a foundation offers a separate legal entity with very few restrictions on its use.

This does not eliminate the need to thoroughly review the tax implications in your country of residence but it does allow you to potentially eliminate or reduce any overseas tax implications and conduct your overseas affairs with minimal overseas disclosure.

Using Offshore Companies/Foundations to Save Tax

Most tax havens, including Panama, St Kitts Nevis, the British Virgin Islands and the Bahamas, do not tax their own IBCs on any income generated from business activities conducted outside that jurisdiction (or any capital gains generated from investments outside that country).

You could therefore use such a structure to trade financial assets such as shares, bonds or futures or to hold property or collect royalties and investment income.

A common structure is to use a combination of an IBC, foundation and trust to avoid capital gains tax. In terms of the countries used you could use a Panama foundation coupled with an offshore company established in an overseas jurisdiction (for example, the Bahamas, St Kitts, the BVI, or Cyprus) and an offshore trust established in another jurisdiction such as the Channel Islands.

This would involve an offshore IBC whose shares are owned by a foundation. The trust would then be the sole beneficiary of the foundation and would list all of the beneficiaries.

This structure could allow you to invest overseas (via the offshore IBC) without being subject to capital gains taxes.

The main purpose of the foundation and trust in this arrangement would be to break the ownership link between you and the offshore IBC.

If you owned the offshore IBC directly it would be likely to fall within most countries' CFC rules and, as such, would be subject to tax. The use of the foundation and trust would make it more difficult for the CFC rules to apply. However, your particular domestic tax legislation may contain specific provisions that tackle this – that's why you need to take detailed tax advice from a tax specialist in your home country.

In the UK for instance, although the foundation and trust may help in arguing that the central management and control of the company is not in the UK, you may still face an S720 problem, and this would therefore need to be considered, in particular if you transfer assets to the offshore IBC.

CHAPTER 6

HOW AN OFFSHORE COMPANY CAN HELP YOU

We know that there are lots of different tax havens that can be used to set up an offshore company such as an IBC. But what exactly are the benefits and in what circumstances are offshore companies used?

In the pages that follow I will illustrate the wide variety of uses to which an offshore IBC can be put. If any of these apply to you, the first step should be to obtain advice from a suitably qualified tax specialist.

Trading Companies

With the breaking down of many trading barriers and the ease of international communications, including the growth of the internet, it truly is a global market out there. More businesses are therefore looking to spread their wings and expand overseas.

In these situations, some significant tax-planning benefits can be obtained.

A simple step is to incorporate an offshore company to form part of your trading group. This would principally be used to purchase or resell goods between the group companies.

So international trading companies could use this set up to establish a re-invoicing strategy and accumulate profits in a low-tax jurisdiction.

Common choices to base an offshore trading company would be Cyprus, Ireland and the Isle of Man in the EU and, further afield, Panama, the BVI and the Bahamas.

Professional Services Companies

Certain individuals providing professional services often use offshore companies. This is partly for asset protection reasons (they are worried about being sued) and partly for tax-planning purposes.

Such individuals include:

- Lawyers
- Doctors
- Designers
- Consultants
- Entertainers

These individuals can often achieve some considerable tax savings by setting up an offshore company.

How does this work? Well in essence the offshore company can enter into a contract with the individual to provide services for clients outside his country of residence. This could then enable personal income to be accumulated free from tax in the offshore jurisdiction.

If the offshore company was to reinvest the money in a tax-free jurisdiction this could enable future income to be generated free of tax.

Example

Steve, a freelance computer programmer is UK resident and UK domiciled. As a UK resident he'll be taxed in the UK on his worldwide income.

But Steve, being a canny chap, uses a Bahamas IBC to bill some of his clients for work that he actually carries out overseas during his various international contracts.

There are some hoops he'll have to jump through in terms of ensuring that the company does not get classed as a UK-resident company (and therefore itself fall within the UK tax net) and avoiding the anti-avoidance rules. However, these can often be overcome and the end result would be that Steve can divert income offshore that would otherwise have been paid to him personally and which then falls outside the scope of UK taxes.

Note that if Steve was to transfer funds to the UK from the offshore company to his personal account (or for his personal benefit) there would then be a UK tax charge.

Using an Offshore Property Company

Investing in property using offshore companies has become increasingly popular as more investors look at investing in overseas property.

The principal advantages of investing via an offshore company are to:

- Avoid inheritance taxes
- Avoid capital gains tax
- Provide the opportunity for a future sale of shares, rather than the underlying property

The procedure is actually remarkably simple. You or the offshore company obtain the funds (usually via a mortgage) which are then used to purchase the property in the name of the IBC.

In terms of you providing funds to the IBC, a straightforward loan would be a good option, depending on the domestic tax legislation. The amount loaned to the IBC could then be extracted tax free in the future.

The rental income would probably not be taxed in the offshore IBC (provided a jurisdiction such as Panama, the Bahamas, or the British Virgin Islands is chosen), however the rental income will often still be taxed in the country where the property is located.

Any tax charge here can usually be minimized by the payment of interest by the IBC, which should be a tax-deductible expense.

Therefore rather than paying cash for a property, the company usually obtains finance for the purchase, from an offshore lender, and the interest payable would further reduce any tax charges.

In the UK using an offshore company to own assets is also popular from an inheritance tax perspective. This is because owning UK assets via an offshore company can enable the UK assets to be taken out of the estate of a non-UK domiciliary.

Example

Elle, a lifelong resident of Canada, is looking to invest in UK investment property. If she purchases the property in her own name this will constitute a UK asset for inheritance tax purposes and, as such, on her death UK probate would be required in addition to a potential tax payment.

If she uses an offshore company to hold the property instead, she will then own shares in an overseas company (a foreign asset) as opposed to a UK property. The shares would not fall into the UK inheritance tax net.

In terms of income tax and capital gains tax, the position of the offshore company would be similar to owning the property personally as a non-resident:

- UK income tax would be levied on the rental profits
- The company would not be taxed on any gain arising when the property is sold.

If you were considering becoming resident in the country where the property is located (for example, retiring there), this will further increase the benefits of using an offshore company to purchase the property before obtaining residence.

By purchasing the property before obtaining residence, it's usually easier to sustain the company's non-resident status and the tax benefits that go with it (in particular, capital gains tax benefits).

If you are both resident and domiciled in the UK, the opportunities to make property investments using offshore companies are more restricted.

Example 2

Let's say Daisy (UK resident and domiciled) wants to buy a property in Bulgaria. She decides to purchase the property via an offshore IBC located in the British Virgin Islands (BVI). The BVI company will own the Bulgarian property but Daisy will own all the shares in the company.

As far as UK tax goes, as a UK domiciliary she would still be subject to UK inheritance tax on her worldwide estate. This would include the Bulgarian property.

If Daisy carefully structures the BVI company so that it is non-UK resident (for example, if she ensures there are overseas directors actually exercising control overseas) the company would be able to dispose of the property free of any UK capital gains tax. Similarly the company would not be subject to income tax on any rental income, as the income is overseas income of a non-resident company.

However as Daisy is UK resident and domiciled, anti-avoidance provisions would apply and any gain on which the company would normally be taxed if it was UK resident will be taxed in her hands.

Similarly, S720 can apply to offshore companies as well as to trusts. This means that the rental income earned by the BVI company could also be taxed in Daisy's hands, unless one of the exemptions applies (for example, if the company is not used to avoid UK tax).

So for UK tax purposes, both UK capital gains tax and income tax could be paid by Daisy on the company's gains and income.

As well as the UK tax, the company will may have to pay Bulgarian withholding taxes on its rental income.

However, the UK taxman would allow Daisy to deduct any Bulgarian tax she pays from her UK tax – so the overall effect is that Daisy will be subject to UK tax on all the income and gains of the BVI company.

Of course if she wanted to avoid tax when she sold the property, she could also become non-resident and dispose of the shares in the BVI company. Given that Bulgarian property is typically purchased by non-residents via a company, there could be a good market in such company disposals. As a non-UK resident, Daisy would then be outside the scope of UK CGT, provided her absence abroad lasts for more than five complete tax years.

You would have to be careful, though, and thoroughly review the overseas country's tax rules. Portugal and Spain, for example, have rules that actually penalise property purchased via an offshore company by incurring an extra tax charge based on a percentage of the property's value.

Investing or Doing Business in Eastern Europe

Many people are now looking to trade or invest in Eastern Europe, which is braced for a long period of economic growth and development.

A key concern will be extracting cash tax-efficiently from these countries particularly where a locally incorporated company has been used (for local planning or regulatory reasons). The withholding taxes on dividend and interest from East European countries will then be a significant issue.

A popular option here is to establish an offshore company in Cyprus, which has double tax treaties with Bulgaria, the Czech Republic, Hungary, Poland, Romania, Russia and Yugoslavia.

These treaties are pretty unusual in the sense that they are the only treaties the East European countries have with a tax haven country.

We've already looked at the benefits of Cyprus and this is therefore another reason why Cyprus offshore companies are ideal vehicles to extract income such as dividends, interest and royalties from East European countries with minimum tax being paid.

The tax agreements Cyprus has with these countries often stipulate a low or 0% withholding tax which, combined with the low taxes in Cyprus, makes this a highly effective set up. Cyprus is often used to hold shares in a Russian trading company, for example, to allow dividends and royalties to be extracted with only a 5% withholding tax.

Offshore Royalty and Patent Companies

If you have designed a new process or product you could consider using an offshore company. The offshore company could purchase the right to use a patent by you and be given the right to license it to other interested parties.

The offshore company can then enter into agreements with licensees around the world who may then manufacture or otherwise use your patent allowing a tax-free roll-up of funds offshore.

Often royalties paid out of a high-tax area attract withholding taxes at source. In many cases using a holding company may allow a reduction in the amount of tax withheld at source.

Again, Cyprus is another popular EU choice here and a patent could be assigned to a Cyprus offshore company allowing it to exploit the rights and benefit from the nil or 5% withholding tax for royalties stipulated in most of the Cyprus double tax treaties.

Other countries that are popular locations for holding patents and copyrights include The Netherlands, the UK, Madeira, Cyprus and Mauritius.

Avoiding Inheritance Tax

Today's internationally mobile individuals often have properties or other assets located worldwide. A common planning technique is to hold these via an offshore personal investment company. This has advantages that in certain countries (the UK being a prime example) non domiciliaries would not be subject to inheritance tax on the value of the property.

This also has practical benefits in that it ensures that on death the property is passed on in accordance with the deceased's wishes and without long bureaucratic procedures in different countries with different inheritance laws.

It is also much easier to transfer shares in the holding company to the chosen heir. So, in Dubai for instance, in order to avoid any issues of forced succession as regards local property, overseas property investors would typically use a company to purchase the Dubai property, and then leave the shares in the company to their family.

Investment Companies

Using an offshore company could also be considered if you have international investments.

An offshore company can invest funds worldwide. Although generally returns or interest payable are subject to local taxation, there are a number of ways to avoid or greatly reduce the taxation using tax-free bonds, bank deposits that pay interest gross and double tax treaties.

Another aspect for investments will be potential capital gains tax on sale. Luckily most offshore companies will be exempt from capital gains tax in the tax haven concerned (as practically all the tax havens covered in this book contain some form of CGT exemption).

If you're looking at investing in the EU, you should also see Chapter 9 on the impact of the EU Savings Tax Directive.

Employment Companies

Often, particularly with the growth of e-commerce, there are individuals trading via companies incorporated in a high-tax country who are looking to live offshore.

One option for them to 'have their cake and eat it' is to use an offshore employment company. Using this they would move overseas and become an employee of the offshore IBC. The IBC would charge the trading company in the home country for the services provided (which should be tax deductible) and the IBC would accumulate income-tax free. This could then be extracted by the proprietor.

Multinationals use this on a larger scale and use offshore employment companies as a vehicle to provide expatriate staff, working outside both their home country and the IBC country, with almost tax-free remuneration.

Example

Cedric lives in Spain and owns his own Spanish trading company (Spainco). He has had enough of the high taxes and decides to move to Cyprus, a fellow EU member. Spainco will continue to be subject to Spanish tax, however Cedric can now charge the company a market rate for his services. These payments would be a tax-deductible expense for Spainco.

Assuming Spainco has trading income of €500,000, if it paid €300,000 to Cedric's offshore company (Cyprus IBC) Spainco would then have taxable profits of only €200,000. The €300,000 paid to Cyprus IBC would be subject to significantly lower rates of tax (typically 10%).

Best Places for Offshore Companies

You are literally spoilt for choice when considering where to incorporate an offshore company. The table below looks purely at the tax rates applicable to some of the more popular offshore IBCs.

Country	Corporate tax rate %
Bermuda	0
Cayman Islands	0
Channel Islands	0
Isle of Man	0
Cyprus	10
Barbados	1
Vanuatu	0
Bahamas	0
British Virgin Islands	0
Nevis	0
Anguilla	0
Ireland	12.5
Gibraltar*	0
Panama*	

*Note in these countries the 0% rate only applies to foreign-sourced income.

The following is a list of the most popular locations for offshore companies together with the key factors to consider:

Anguilla

- No corporate taxes on company profits
- Tax exempt for 50 years
- Flexible company name rules

The Bahamas

- No corporate taxes on company profits
- Excellent selection of local professionals
- Long-standing reputation as a stable offshore provider
- Guaranteed tax exemption for 20 years

Bermuda

- No corporate taxes on company profits
- Does require disclosure to tax authorities
- Investment income derived from abroad may be taxed
- Relatively expensive place to incorporate

British Virgin Islands

- Politically stable established destination (over 300,000 IBCs)
- No corporate taxes for a non-resident company
- Fast and low-cost company incorporation

Cayman Islands

- Long-established offshore infrastructure
- Exempt companies pay no corporate taxes
- Exempt for 20 years

Cyprus

- Full EU member

• Large number of double tax treaties (48 at the last count) which provide for reduced or 0% withholding taxes on dividends, interest and royalties paid to a Cyprus company
• Excellent banking and commercial infrastructure
• Low incorporation and ongoing fees
• Beneficial ownership is disclosed to the Central Bank of Cyprus only, which is bound by secrecy
• Non-resident companies pay corporate tax at 10% only on income derived in Cyprus

Isle of Man

• Well developed professional and financial infrastructure
• Disclosure to local tax authorities
• A new 0% rate of corporation tax
• Handy for UK expats as filing etc is all in English

Labuan

• One of the leading offshore centres in Asia
• Well-developed financial and professional infrastructure
• No tax for a non-trading exempt company and only 3% or RM20,000 (around $5,000) if the company is trading
• Can claim alternative treatment and avoid tax on overseas trading income
• Disclosure to tax authorities required

Liechtenstein

• Politically stable
• Strong banking and financial services
• High levels of privacy and strict confidentiality laws
• Close ties with Switzerland
• Joint stock companies are exempt from income tax, property tax (with the exception for real estate) and capital gains tax.

St Kitts and Nevis

• The major source of revenue is tourism followed by offshore financial services
• St Kitts Nevis LLC (limited liability company) can be used for any business venture or professional practice anywhere in the world outside St

Kitts
- Combines the corporate advantages of limited liability with the partnership advantages of pass-through taxation
- No St Kitts tax for non-residents

Panama

- One of the oldest offshore centres in the world
- Strong secrecy laws
- Minimal reporting requirements
- Bearer shares can be issued
- No tax for non-residents

Which One is Best?

This is the $64,000 question and, not surprisingly, the answer is not clear cut.

A lot depends on the purpose to which the company is put and the country in which you will be resident.

If you want to trade in China, for example, a Cayman or Mauritian company could be ideal. If maximum asset protection is required, a St Kitts company is often a good choice because the authorities require a $25,000 bond to be put up before a plaintiff can have a suit filed. This clearly puts off many litigants.

However, a good overall offering is the Panamanian IBC. The combination of low set-up expenses, zero taxation and a stable economy is hard to beat.

In addition it offers a guaranteed exemption from Panamanian taxes provided income is derived outside Panama. Other countries such as the Bahamas and Belize offer similar guarantees, however they have limits to the tax-exempt status (typically 15 to 20 years).

Panama offers a permanent exemption, which makes it more suitable for long-term tax planning.

Finally, many offshore IBCs have limits as to the business that the IBC can carry out. For example, a Bahamas IBC company cannot engage in business with Bahamians or own property in the Bahamas. By contrast a Panama Company has none of these problems.

If you're looking at international trading you'd be looking at countries that have a good double-tax treaty network and a low rate of tax – Ireland and Cyprus are good choices.

It's also worth remembering that all of the countries will be affected by the new information sharing provisions as outlined by the OECD. However, as has been reiterated in other parts of the book, if you're using the offshore company to avoid tax you should be adhering to the disclosure requirements in your home country anyway.

Using Protected/Segregated Cell Companies

Over the past few years a new form of corporate entity has been developed in a number of offshore jurisdictions. Places such as the Seychelles, Bermuda and the Channel Islands have introduced the concept of the segregated or protected cell company. It was primarily designed for the offshore insurance market but creative tax planners have adapted it to other situations, such as trading or property investment.

With this setup there is a single parent company – the segregated cell company (SCC) – within which there are subdivisions called 'cells'. This means there are two distinct 'layers' to the company – the SCC itself and the underlying cells.

The SCC has its own assets, which are non-cellular and separate from the individual cells.

Each cell is an independent entity capable of operating separately from all other cells. Importantly there is a segregation of the assets contained within the cell. This is important in terms of asset protection, as creditors of one cell can't look to the assets of another cell, or of the company. There is, therefore, a complete segregation of assets and liabilities of each cell.

Crucially, though, in legal terms there is still only one company and one legal entity.

Each cell is identified by a unique name and can issue shares ('cell shares'). The proceeds of the issue of cell shares are classed as cell share capital, whereas the proceeds of the issue of shares other than cell shares are classed as the company's non-cellular assets.

A protected cell company may pay a dividend (known as a 'cellular dividend') in respect of cell shares.

A cell company is therefore one legal entity that has protected and distinct 'layers' or cells. Its main benefit is in terms of asset protection.
An alternative to a cell company is to have a number of subsidiary companies. The downside to this is the risk that a claim may flow from one asset of one company and affect another one.

Cell Companies and Their Uses

Many property developers looking to develop multiple properties have traditionally used a separate subsidiary company for each development. This has a few disadvantages, especially in terms of tax, however the overall aim is to protect the group.
Given the litigious nature of property development, having each development in a separate entity makes sense.

Another option, though, would be to use a segregated cell company, with each cell undertaking a different development. This would achieve the asset protection advantages while minimising the costs and admin burden.

You could also use the cell company for trading purposes, eg to hold different trades within the same company.

Tax Implications

Given that there is no specific guidance on the use of these entities and how they fit within the tax regime in many developed countries, I've set out some of the uses and opportunities that could be considered. Clearly, though, you will have to review the implications in your home country jurisdiction in detail.

Here are some of a cell company's potential advantages:

Tax Returns

As the cell company is the only legal entity there may only be a requirement to submit one tax return.

Associated Companies

To get separate legal protection for two or more activities you would usually form separate corporations to carry out each activity. In some tax regimes, each corporation would be 'associated' for tax purposes with the other companies. This would result in a splitting up of the available tax bands. This could easily lead to an increase in the rate of corporation tax payable. For example, instead of paying 20% tax on up to £300,000 of profits, the company would pay 20% on only £150,000 and tax at a higher rate on the remainder.

Using a cell company could potentially eliminate this associated company tax problem.

Losses

If you use a cell company to carry on completely separate activities within the same legal entity, in many jurisdictions you should be able to offset the losses of one cell against the profits of another.

Asset Transfers

Assets should be able to be transferred within the company with no tax implications. This is unlike the position that applies to groups of companies where there are lots of anti-avoidance provisions that could apply.

In this case there is only one legal entity and the transfer of an asset within this is not taxed in many jurisdictions.

Residency Provisions

This is an even more aggressive interpretation of the provisions. Under normal circumstances an offshore company is resident in a country if it is controlled from there.

What if a segregated cell company had non-cellular shareholders overseas? These shareholders would actually control the activities of the company and, as such, the company should be non-resident.

For example, one of the cells could invest in UK property or other assets, and on the basis that it was non-resident it would be exempt from UK tax on any gain arising.

In terms of managing the particular cell, it may be possible to argue that a director of the cell was not controlling the company, and therefore having a

UK resident director of the property investment cell may not affect the non-residency status. While there would be other provisions to consider (eg anti-avoidance rules) the potential benefits are clear.

Step by Step Guide to Setting up Your IBC

You will almost certainly use an incorporation agent who will take care of all the paperwork for you. However, you too need to know about the various procedures involved so you understand exactly what is happening and what you are signing.

The information below is a general guide. The actual procedure and what you can and cannot do will vary between tax havens (for example, as to whether bearer shares can be issued, the minimum number of directors and whether you can use nominees).

However, the following list will give you a useful insight into how a company is set up:

Step 1

The first step will be choosing the country in which to form your IBC. Hopefully, after reading this book, you will have some idea as to which country is best for you. You'll have to take into account not just the tax environment of your chosen country but also what the company will be used for, the setup and ongoing costs, and privacy and confidentiality issues.

Step 2

Next, you'll need to think about the type of entity that you want to form. Many offshore jurisdictions will offer different types of IBC companies, for example exempt companies, non-resident companies, holding companies, as well as other entities such as LLPs and LLCs.

With respect to IBCs the key differences will usually be in terms of filing requirements and annual fees but you should ask your incorporation agent about the differences between the various types of entity.

Step 3

Next you will need to choose your company's name. You've got pretty much a free rein here although you'll need to be guided by your incorporation agent to ensure that the name does not break any restrictions in the country of incorporation. Note that if you form a ready made company, you will need to change the name of the company to one that you want.

Step 4

Next the articles of association will need to be drafted. These are basically the rules that govern the operation of the company and are often provided by your incorporation agent in the form of standard pro forma documents. You could however draft customized ones if preferred. However for most people the standard articles should be fine.

Step 5

You will then need to think about the share capital and method of funding. When you form your company you may need to transfer some money into the company. There are essentially two different ways to do this, either as a loan or as share capital. The advantage of a loan is that it allows a tax-free extraction of funds in the future by way of a loan repayment.

Note that many developed countries (for example, the UK) have special rules (known as 'thin capitalisation' rules) that prevent overseas individuals forming companies with low share capital and large loans.

Because interest on loans is tax deductible, but dividends on shares are not, overseas companies could gain an easy tax advantage by forming UK subsidiaries with large loan accounts. The taxman therefore restricts the tax deductibility of interest unless the debt/equity ratio of the company is realistic (in other words, would a third party bank lend the funds to the company in question?). Of course for the nil-tax offshore jurisdictions the thin capitalisation rules will not be an issue if there is no tax charged on the profits.

When we're looking at share capital usually the amount that you initially subscribe is low (for example, $100) and this nominal share capital bears no relation to the underlying value of the company.

For example, a $1 share could easily be worth $10,000 – the value of the share will depend on the level of assets and profitability of the company.

Step 6

There are various types of shares (or, more correctly, classes of share) that could be issued by the company and you'll need to decide which shares your company will issue.

These include:

Bearer shares – These are shares that give the holder of the share certificate the rights of ownership. In theory if you lose the share certificates you would then lose the ownership over those shares.

The benefit in issuing bearer shares is that there is no disclosure of the real owner's name in the shareholders' register. This makes bearer shares ideal where anonymity is important.

In practice, bearer share certificates aren't issued in many non-offshore jurisdictions (and where they are, the share certificates are usually kept in a locked safe). So bearer shares are not permitted in the UK, US, Australia, Cyprus, Barbados and Singapore. All shares in these jurisdictions must be registered.

Many jurisdictions do, however, permit bearer shares, including:

- The British Virgin Islands
- The Cayman Islands
- Switzerland
- Liechtenstein
- Panama
- The Bahamas
- Austria
- Germany
- Costa Rica

The advantage of bearer shares is that they offer excellent privacy. However, the same rights and responsibilities apply to this type of share as to any other and just because the shares are held as bearer shares doesn't alter the tax position. You would still be liable to tax on either any dividends received or on a gain on disposal, subject to the tax rules of your country of residence.

Preference shares – These usually offer the shareholder a fixed dividend receipt paid in preference to ordinary shareholders. They do not usually give owners the right to vote on company affairs.

Class A & B shares – Having different classes of share allows you to give different rights and benefits to different groups of shareholders.

You could, for example, grant class A shares to be held by you with full voting and dividend rights and class B shares with no voting rights but full dividend rights to be held by someone else. These could be gifted or subscribed for by your children, allowing an entitlement to income with no influence on the operation of the company.

Step 7

Of crucial importance is deciding who will be the directors of the company. You'll need to ensure that the minimum number of directors is met (usually 2-3). Often it will be you and your wife or other family members/business partners who will be acting as directors.

If you're looking at establishing an offshore IBC you may need to consider using the services of nominees to act as directors.

A lot of the offshore incorporation agents will try and convince you to use them for this purpose. Aside from the fact that they will charge you for this service, you need to realise that they will have control over your company.

If you're keen to establish that the company is controlled from overseas a good option is to arrange for the company to be owned by an offshore trust, with control passed to a professional trust management company.

You could then be a beneficiary of the trust and, provided the trust exercised control overseas, the company could be argued to be non-resident.

If required, the trustees could even act as directors of the company. This would make it easier to establish the company as non-resident.

How Long Does it Take to Set Up a Company?

This will depend on the country in question and will vary from between one week and one month.

You'll often be offered an off-the-shelf corporation as a fast option. You need to be careful here as you do not know the company's history. In other words, whether the company was engaged in something that will come back to bite you later on.

Given that the incorporation process is usually pretty straightforward it usually makes sense to incorporate from scratch.

How Much Does it Cost to Set Up an Offshore Company?

As you'd expect, the cost will vary tremendously depending on which country you choose and which incorporation agent you use. You'll be looking at an IBC in Costa Rica or Panama for as little as £500. By contrast, incorporating in Bermuda will cost you several thousand pounds.

You need to be careful as there are a number of offshore formation firms and lawyers that charge outrageous amounts of money to set up and maintain both foundation, trust and IBC structures. Some of these prices are way out of line but most people do not know any better and end up paying quite a bit.

As with everything, do your research before committing yourself.

CHAPTER 7

HOW BIG COMPANIES AND THE RICH USE TAX HAVENS

Tax havens are also of great use to companies, as well as individuals. In fact, some of the world's largest multinationals such as Pepsi and News International use offshore tax haven structures to minimize the overall amount of tax they pay.

Of course, the big multinationals have teams of highly paid tax advisers whose job it is to ferret out tax-saving opportunities around the globe. Broadly speaking there are two distinct ways they use tax havens to slash a company's overall tax rate.

This overall tax rate (also known as the effective tax rate) is simply the total tax paid by the company divided by its profits.

The first way they reduce their taxes is by 'corporate migration'. The second way is by using tax haven subsidiaries.

Corporate Migration

This is the most straightforward option and at its most simple means that a company transfers its headquarters to an offshore tax haven. This could either be a total transfer of operations, a part transfer of operations or sometimes the transfer would be in name only without the actual operations being moved.

You'll need to be careful when doing this, as many developed countries won't be fooled by a transfer in name only. You would actually need to transfer physical operations, which in itself could lead to a further tax charge.

In practice what you often see is a part transfer of operations with, for example, back-office functions and even some front line services (for example, call centres and customer services functions) being transferred overseas.

The tax savings come about because in many tax havens companies do not have to pay taxes on their overseas operations. As always, detailed professional advice is required to ensure that the residence of the company is actually transferred.

Using Tax Haven Subsidiaries

This is really where the teams of tax accountants that the large multinationals have on tap come into their own.

The use of offshore subsidiaries is big business – Enron, for example had over 600, many just existing in name only.

This is a complex area and the uses of these companies will obviously depend on the jurisdictions involved, types of business and so on. However, as an illustration here are some of the most popular strategies:

Deferring Tax Payments

A number of countries, such as the US, tax resident companies on their worldwide profits but also allow a deferral of tax for any profits generated from overseas operations, provided the profits are reinvested overseas. This therefore allows corporate groups based in these countries to use tax haven subsidiaries to hold overseas trading operations and reduce the overall tax charge.

Income Stripping/Offshore Finance Companies

This idea is developed below but essentially involves a tax haven subsidiary lending money to a tax paying company. The interest charged on the loans is then allowable as a tax deduction for the tax paying company but should be subject to low or no tax in the tax haven company.

Offshore Intellectual Property

Similar to the above, a tax paying company would transfer intellectual property (this is a very wide term and includes patents, copyright, know-how and goodwill) to a tax haven subsidiary. The tax haven company can then charge a licensing fee for the use of the intellectual property.

The income from any overseas subsidiaries that pay the tax haven company for using the intellectual property would then not be taxable in the hands of the tax paying company.

In addition, and in a similar way to income stripping above, the tax haven company can charge the tax paying company and these charges should be tax deductible for the tax paying company (a double benefit arises as there would be both a tax deduction on payment and no tax payable on receipt).

Transfer Pricing

This used to be a major opportunity but some of the larger industrialised countries now have strict transfer-pricing legislation.

Transfer pricing simply means the rate charged for good and services between connected parties, such as between a parent company and subsidiaries.

The aim with any effective transfer pricing strategy would be to arrange the group structure so that tax paying companies are paying management charges or other inter-company service charges to tax haven group companies. Provided the paying company gets a tax deduction for the amount paid, the group would be significantly better off.

This would typically also apply to purchases of stock or parts from overseas or intercompany salaries charged for using overseas staff. The mark-up would enable an increased tax deduction for the company that pays the management charge in the high tax country.

Note that it's essential that the paying company gets a tax deduction for the payments in order for this to be tax effective.

Nowadays companies need to be careful that transfer pricing legislation does not apply to require an arm's length rate to be used. The UK, for example, has some strict transfer-pricing provisions that will effectively only allow a tax deduction in these circumstances for the market value of the services provided. If this applied it would then negate the benefit of the high transfer price.

Restructuring

One of the ways that the larger UK corporate groups look to achieve the benefits of migration is by creating an offshore holding company.

They try to achieve this by interposing a new non-UK holding company between the UK company and its shareholders. The shareholders would then own shares in a non-resident company, which then owns the UK company.

This is relatively straightforward and can be achieved by a share for share exchange provided the share exchange is accepted as being for bona fide commercial purposes. If not then you would be looking at further reorganising to implement the holding company.

You would need to ensure that the holding company was genuinely managed from abroad to ensure it was not UK resident and was exempt from UK corporation tax on overseas income.

The key advantage in having an offshore holding company is that:

- It can receive overseas income streams generally free of UK tax, and
- It can hold shares in CFCs without being subject to the onerous CFC provisions.

In addition, using this type of restructuring avoids a possible exit for the UK company as it would still be controlled from the UK, but the shareholders can obtain the benefits of offshore company tax treatment.

Using Holding Companies

Holding companies are often used as a form of financial funnel. By having a company located in a suitable holding company jurisdiction hold the shares in a variety of companies, it's possible to ensure that the profits are funnelled into a low tax, or tax advantageous environment.

In order to be effective there are a number of prerequisites that a holding company and subsidiary must satisfy, in particular an ability to avoid withholding taxes.

Ability to Avoid Withholding Taxes & CGT

Most developed countries impose some type of withholding tax on dividends, interest or royalties sent overseas by companies.

This usually works a bit like PAYE for employees. When an employee receives salary an amount has already been deducted and paid to the tax authorities by the employer.

In other words, the payer has accounted for tax on behalf of the recipient.

The same applies to withholding taxes. The payer company will complete any required forms and withhold tax from the payment on behalf of the recipient.

The recipient who has suffered the withholding tax will need to look at the domestic tax legislation to identify whether any tax relief can be claimed.

Some countries such as the UK and the US automatically allow a measure of relief for any overseas tax paid when calculating the recipient's local tax liability.

This is where double tax treaties really come in handy. Certain treaties will allow payments between participating states to be made free of withholding tax or at least at reduced rates.

This could therefore allow dividends, interest and royalties to be passed between the holding company and subsidiary companies without any tax being deducted.

Of course, there may be tax on the receipt of the dividend in the holding company, depending on the local tax regime.

"Why not then base the holding company in a tax haven to avoid all taxes?" is a question many people ask.

Well, in principle this is sound, the problem is that most tax haven countries do not have any double tax treaties, and where they do they are not the standard OECD treaty giving withholding tax relief. Therefore you would be subject to the full rates of withholding taxes.

The trick therefore is to find a country that has the tax treaty benefits with a favourable domestic tax regime for the holding company.

Another point to bear in mind is capital gains tax (CGT). The holding company will be doing just that – holding shares in a variety of subsidiary companies.

What if someone comes along and offers to buy one of the subsidiary companies?

The holding company needs to ensure that it's not located in a regime that is going to tax it heavily on the capital gain. Therefore any profits attributable to the holding company when it sells any subsidiaries should be subject to no (or low) taxes.

Another issue mainly for the large multinationals is that the holding company may simply itself be an intermediate company. You may, for example, have a Parent company owning holding companies 1,2 and 3 who then in turn own various subsidiaries.

In this case, holding companies 1, 2 and 3 are all holding companies but they are themselves owned by the parent company (the 'top' company is sometimes known as the 'ultimate holding company').

This is a common structure for multinational groups mainly because the structure of the group can be aligned with the geographical location of the businesses or according to the industries the group operates in.

So, for example, Holding Company 1 may hold all the companies trading in Europe, Holding Company 2 may hold all the companies trading in the US, and so on. Alternatively, Holding Company 1 may hold the trading companies involved in the manufacture of widgets, while the other holding companies own shares in trading companies involved in other industries.

You'll therefore see a flow of cash from the trading companies to the holding companies and finally up to the parent company in the form of dividends or by way of other charges (for example, royalties or management charges).

Anyone using such a structure would need to ensure firstly that dividends paid by a holding company to the parent company are either exempt from or subject to low withholding tax in the holding company's jurisdiction.

Secondly, low or zero capital gains tax on disposal of the shares by the parent company would be important.

Seeing that one of the main attractions of a holding company is its ability to receive dividend payments with little or no tax deducted and that typical tax haven companies often do not fit this purpose (due to the lack of double tax treaties), which countries are the best place to locate holding companies?

Denmark

Denmark is a highly attractive location for holding companies. Being part of the EU, it's subject to the EU's Parent-Subsidiary directive. This means that where a Danish holding company controls at least 25% of the shares of another EU subsidiary, any dividends paid by the subsidiary to the Danish holding company will not have withholding tax deducted.

As a back-up, Denmark also has lots of double tax treaties (approximately 60) to reduce the rates of withholding tax on dividends received by Danish holding companies from non-EU countries, or where the EU directive doesn't apply.

Avoiding withholding taxes is just one aspect. Of crucial importance is the tax treatment in Denmark itself. The Danish corporate income tax rate is 25% but there is special legislation that exempts dividends received by a Danish holding company, provided various conditions are satisfied. Where this applies there's no tax in Denmark, even if tax has not been paid by the subsidiary that paid the dividend.

This makes Denmark unusual in the EU as the other key holding company jurisdictions (Austria, Belgium, France, Germany, Luxembourg, The Netherlands and the UK) only exempt the dividend income if the foreign subsidiary has already paid tax.

In terms of capital gains tax on the sale of shares by the holding company, the standard CGT rate in Denmark can be up to 25%.

However, again the domestic legislation contains an exemption which can ensure that no CGT is charged on the gains that a holding company makes when it disposes of an overseas subsidiary.

Therefore, Denmark offers a highly attractive regime for locating a holding company and is often considered the benchmark offshore holding company jurisdiction.

In terms of tax on dividend income, the combination of Denmark's double tax treaty network and its holding company regime means that it offers some serious advantages and there are currently approximately 35 countries which can route their dividends through Denmark without paying any withholding taxes. This combined with the CGT exemption means it is one of the top holding company destinations.

Belgium

Belgium is another popular location for holding companies. The principal advantage is on the capital gains tax front. Where a Belgian holding company disposes of shares in a subsidiary, the gain it realises can be completely exempt from Belgian CGT. This is similar to the position of Danish holding companies, however in actual fact it's even more beneficial. This is because the Danish holding companies are subject to more restrictions that do not apply to Belgian companies (for example, the holding company would need to hold the shares for at least three years).

United Kingdom

The UK is often overlooked as a holding country location, although it does offer some excellent opportunities. For a start the UK has more double tax treaties than all of its main competitors. Given the quality and extent of the treaty network, it is often said to be the best country for extracting overseas dividends at the lowest tax cost.

The UK will also allow the shareholder to claim a tax credit for any 'underlying tax'. This is the tax the company has already paid before paying the dividend (for example, the company's corporation tax charge). In order to claim credit for underlying tax, the shareholder must own at least 10% of the shares in the company.

This therefore means that where the underlying foreign corporate tax rate is 21% or more (for 2014/15), this credit will normally mean total relief from UK corporation tax. So it's therefore effectively the same as an exemption in these circumstances. Also bear in mind that the UK has lower rates of corporation tax than most other industrial nations.

There have, however, been provisions introduced to simplify this system in 2009. In essence overseas dividends received by a UK company could qualify for a complete tax exemption.

The UK is also pretty unusual in that it doesn't impose any withholding tax on dividends distributed by UK companies to UK non-resident shareholders. So non-resident shareholders can usually extract funds from a UK company free of UK income tax.

There are also capital gains tax benefits to UK holding companies. Where they are part of a trading group, new substantial shareholding legislation should apply to exempt any gain arising in full.

Finally, it's also very cheap to set up and run a UK holding company.

Using Holding Companies to Own Tax Haven Subsidiaries

If you're looking to establish overseas companies in nil-tax jurisdictions, it's also important to consider whether the holding company jurisdiction has any special provisions that apply to dividends from tax-haven jurisdictions. Some of the preferred jurisdictions in this case are:

Malaysia

When considering Malaysia you would usually use a Malaysian holding company that is 100% owned by an offshore Labuan company.

The scope of Malaysian taxes is limited by the principle of territoriality. This means that any income earned outside Malaysia is exempt from Malaysian taxes even though it is paid to a Malaysian company.

Therefore, dividend income from an overseas subsidiary would be excluded from Malaysian taxes.

Note that transfers between the Malaysian and Labuan companies would be free of taxes, including withholding taxes.

Any dividends payable to a UK or US shareholder would then be from the Labuan company and would be free of withholding taxes.

Any future disposal of the shares in the subsidiaries by the Malaysian company would again be free of capital gains tax.

Therefore the Malaysian holding company option provides a method of avoiding corporation tax and outgoing withholding taxes.

If the subsidiary jurisdictions did levy withholding taxes (ie they weren't located in nil-tax havens) you'd then need to review any tax treaties. The treaties between Malaysia and the subsidiaries are of crucial importance, however it is fair to say that they are at a disadvantage compared with the European holding companies as they are not entitled to the benefits of the

EU parent/subsidiary directive, which can eliminate withholding taxes on dividends between EU companies.

Switzerland

Swiss companies can be taxed on their income at both federal and canton level. There are, however, specific tax reliefs for Swiss holding companies. Effectively this is a holding company that doesn't conduct business in Switzerland and the deeds of the company specifically state it is a holding company. The net effect of being classed as a holding company is that there is no cantonal tax, and the federal income tax is 8.5%.
There is, however, a participation exemption that applies where the holding company owns more than 20% of the shares in the subsidiary. In this case, dividend income received from the subsidiary is effectively received free of income tax. So importantly, the Swiss holding company should also be effectively tax free for dividend receipts and as there are no controlled foreign companies' regulations, the fact that dividends are received from tax havens would not affect this.

The downside is that the standard Swiss withholding tax rate is 35%. However it does have some treaties, which can reduce this to 5%-15%.

In terms of dividends received by the Swiss company from subsidiaries, you would have to look to the available double-tax treaties. Most treaties apply a 15% treaty rate. However Switzerland has signed an EU agreement so that dividends paid by subsidiary companies to a Swiss holding company are not liable for taxation in the subsidiary country subject to various conditions. This puts Switzerland in the favourable position of being able to receive dividends from EU states free of withholding taxes.

Cyprus

The general rule is that taxable profits of all Cyprus companies are now taxed at the rate of 12.5%. However Cyprus also has a special regime for holding companies.

Dividend income from an overseas subsidiary to a Cypriot holding company is exempt from corporation tax provided the holding company owns at least 1% of the share capital of the subsidiary.

Note that this exemption will not apply if the company paying the dividend engages in more than 50% of its activities in producing investment income

and the foreign tax burden on the income of the company paying the dividends is substantially lower than that in Cyprus.
In this case, the Cyprus company would be taxed at a rate of 15%.

However, provided the overseas subsidiaries are trading, the fact that dividends are from a tax haven would not result in a Cypriot tax charge.

There is no withholding tax on the payment of dividends from Cyprus to a UK or US shareholder and any gain on the sale of the shares would be exempt from corporation tax.

Therefore of key importance are the withholding taxes on the payments to the holding company.

Cyprus has fewer treaties than other jurisdictions such as Denmark or Switzerland but the provisions can be beneficial. Dividends from countries such as Bulgaria, Greece, Ireland, Malta and Russia are subject to reduced withholding taxes.

In addition, as it is party to the EU parent/subsidiary directive, dividends from EU companies should be free of withholding taxes.

So like Switzerland, Cyprus is effective in that it exempts dividends from tax in Cyprus, has no CGT on disposal, and does not impose a withholding tax on outgoing dividends. In terms of incoming dividends it is very efficient as a holding company for Eastern European companies given the number and nature of treaties with these countries. It would, for example, be an effective intermediary holding company for shares in a Russian company. Dividends could pass with reduced withholding taxes to the Cyprus company and then onwards to the ultimate holding company.

Madeira

Madeira has a special regime for holding companies. In terms of domestic taxation, on the receipt of dividends from EU subsidiaries there would be a 100% tax reduction providing an effective tax rate of 0%. Dividends from non-EU subsidiary companies would also not be taxed.

As a party to the EU parent/subsidiary directive any dividends would be received from EU companies free of withholding taxes, and non-EU jurisdictions would be dependent on the terms of relevant double-tax treaties. For example, the Bulgarian treaty provides for 10%/15%

withholding taxes on dividends while the agreement with Germany provides for a fixed 15%.

How can you use the offshore holding company?

It's all very well learning how multinationals benefit from offshore holding companies. But if you're looking at establishing an international business, how can you take advantage of these opportunities?

Some of the possibilities are as follows:

Offshore Finance Company

A common use of the offshore company is as a provider or funds.

If you're looking at establishing a business to trade in the EU or USA for example, you could use an offshore holding company that would provide funds to subsidiaries in various countries so that the subsidiaries obtain the benefit of tax deductions on interest paid.

This is effectively a way of creating a tax deduction that may not otherwise be available. Note you would need to be careful to ensure that any loan was correctly drafted (for example, using suitable loan agreements) and the interest rate is calculated on an arm's length basis.

Example

You've designed a new widget and will be selling it around the world. As well as establishing suitable trading companies onshore, you could take advantage of an offshore holding company to fund the initial set up.

The holding company would obtain the funds (either from a bank or investors) and would lend the funds to the trading subsidiaries. They would then use the funds for the purpose of their trade (for example, the manufacture and sale of new widgets).

Ideally the holding company would be situated offshore in an area where there is no corporation tax and this would allow it to roll up funds tax free. The trading companies should also be entitled to a tax deduction for the interest paid to the holding company, provided this is structured correctly.

This is a win-win scenario as there is a tax deduction, with no corresponding taxable receipt.

Interest payments from group companies may be subject to withholding tax, but these taxes differ from the usual corporation taxes. Many large companies establish their own offshore companies for the purpose of mixing dividends of subsidiaries and deriving maximum advantage from tax credits. This 'pooling' or 'mixing' of income is a complex area and is something that in house tax departments of multinationals look at in considerable detail.

Offshore Patent Holding

If you've designed a new process or product you could consider using an offshore company. The offshore company could purchase the right to use your patent and sublicense it.

The offshore company can then enter into agreements with licensees around the world who may then manufacture or otherwise use your patent allowing a tax-free roll up of funds in the offshore company.

Royalties paid out of a high-tax country often attract withholding taxes at source but in many cases using a holding company may allow a reduction in the rate of tax withheld at source.

Note that the offshore company should acquire the patent as soon as possible to ensure that little value is attributed to it. If possible it should be assigned/sold while still pending, as a gain may well arise on the transfer to the company. If the patent holder is based in a high tax jurisdiction this could represent a substantial gain arising, particularly if the transfer to the overseas company is deemed to be at market value (which would be the case in most high-tax jurisdictions).

Minimizing Risk

This is based on the 'don't place all your eggs in one basket' principle. As some countries suffer from both political and economic instability you may like to follow the example of many large multinationals that move the base of operations and ownership of assets offshore. If you're looking for a sound environment, with excellent political stability, some of the Caribbean jurisdictions may not be top choice. Places like Luxembourg or Bermuda are the favoured jurisdictions.

Avoidance of CGT and Withholding Taxes

As you've seen above, one of the main uses of offshore holding companies is to extract profits free of withholding taxes and CGT. You may be considering investing or trading in a country with which your home country does not have a double tax treaty.

In this case, you may decide to use a holding company in a jurisdiction that does have a suitable double tax treaty. For example, Cyprus has an extensive double tax treaty network with many Eastern European countries and countries of the former Soviet Union, and the use of Cypriot companies for inward investment into these countries is often advised.

You have to be careful as some double tax treaties, in particular US treaties, now have 'limitation of benefits' articles which can restrict treaty benefits (see Chapter 10 on double tax treaties).

CHAPTER 8

PROTECTING YOUR PRIVACY WITH NOMINEES

Using an IBC as a nominee or for re-invoicing purposes are two common uses for offshore companies, so it's worthwhile looking into them in a little more detail.

A nominee arrangement is not really in itself a tax-saving option, although the privacy benefits would mean it could be used in conjunction with other tax-planning structures.

The basic premise is that one of the disadvantages of using an offshore IBC is that the tax authorities in some of the high-tax developed countries may pay close attention to your Cayman Islands or Panamanian IBC.

However, by using a company in an 'onshore' jurisdiction you are less likely to raise suspicion. Of course, there should be nothing to hide in the first place but often it's a case of avoiding long protracted tax enquiries.
This arrangement is really only suitable for a trader.

How Does it Work?

Well, taking the UK as an example, a UK company is incorporated to be used as the nominee company. The UK company acts on behalf of an offshore IBC which is itself based in a tax haven.

This is basically an agency arrangement with the UK company being the 'agent' and the offshore IBC being the 'principal'. Therefore any business that the UK company conducts is on behalf of the tax haven IBC.

The type of activities the UK company could get involved in would include negotiating deals, marketing, administration and so on. The UK company could invoice UK clients for services performed and then pay the cash received to the tax haven company, less a small charge for the services provided.

The tax haven company is effectively kept out of the trading operations and for all intents and purposes the clients deal directly with the UK company. This may also reassure any client companies that may otherwise not want to deal with a tax haven company.

Note that in order for this to be a proper commercial arrangement, the agency company should charge a fee to the tax haven IBC for the provision of its services, and in its accounts the amount of trading income handled on behalf of the offshore IBC would not normally have to be shown.

Given the strict transfer pricing laws in many countries the amount of the fee would need to be carefully considered and based on a market rate – as a rough guide 5% to 15% of the gross turnover. Any expenses of the agency company are set against this and tax will be paid in the UK on the taxable profits. The cash could then be extracted by any non-resident shareholders free of UK income taxes.

The benefit of this arrangement is that a resident company is less likely to be subject to scrutiny than an offshore company based in a tax haven.

Clearly if any enquiries are made by the tax authorities the arrangement should be fully disclosed and provided an arm's length basis is used and adequate documentary evidence is retained to back up the nominee structure, this should alleviate any concerns.

When Can the Agency Structure Be Used?

Trading Operations

This type of arrangement is most relevant to a trading operation and effectively separates the transactions, with the invoicing being done by the agency company and delivery and transfer of title in the goods resting with the offshore IBC.

Note that it's important to distinguish between the invoicing and the generation of profit. Whereas there is no problem with the nominee company invoicing for the services or products provided, any profit actually made should be generated by the tax haven 'principal' company.

Therefore the offshore IBC should actually purchase and dispose of the goods (for example, transfer title) to ensure that any profit is made by the IBC. Provided you've chosen the location of the offshore IBC carefully, no tax should be payable by the IBC. You should also bear in mind that most IBCs aren't allowed to trade in the country where they are incorporated.

Property

You could also use this structure for owning property. In this case the offshore IBC would own the property and the agency company would act as a property management agent.

Rental income is invoiced by the nominee company and received by it on behalf of the offshore IBC. As above, the agency company would charge a commercially acceptable fee to the IBC (calculated on an arm's length basis) which would usually be taxable (less expenses).

The benefits here are that:

- The tenants don't know they are dealing with an offshore IBC.
- Any gain on disposal would arise in the offshore IBC (for example, in the case of the UK, any gain would be exempt if the offshore company is non-UK resident).
- The rental income would be taxed in the hands of the IBC.

Service Companies

The agency structure could also be used where you are supplying services via an offshore company but didn't want these invoices shown in your accounts. This may be the case where for example you move offshore and invoice your trading company for services you provide.

Your Customers

If you are based offshore and provide services to client companies possibly in a high tax jurisdiction, your customers may not like having invoices from a tax haven in their accounts on the basis that the taxman may look into their affairs in a bit more detail.

You could therefore form an agency company in a respectable 'onshore' jurisdiction (for example, the UK) to invoice the client.

Where to Incorporate

This will clearly depend on the use of the agency arrangement and the countries of any trading/property holding.

However, the UK is known as a good choice for the nominee company, given its sound trading reputation and tough anti-money-laundering rules.

In terms of the offshore company – take your pick! The Bahamas, British Virgin Islands and Panama are all favourites.

As you'll see, closely linked with the nominee idea, is the use of a company as a tool for re-invoicing.

Re-invoicing is just the establishment of an offshore IBC to act as an intermediary between a trader and the clients.

It allows profits to be split between onshore and offshore jurisdictions, with the aim obviously being to redirect some of the trading profits to tax haven jurisdictions. Profits could then be accumulated offshore, with hopefully (if structured correctly) the onshore company receiving a tax deduction for the amounts paid to the offshore company.

Example

An international trading company sells €1,000,000 of goods to European customers and earns a gross profit €400,000. It pays tax at 30%, so its tax bill will be €120,000 reducing its net profits to €280,000.

One option the company may consider is establishing a tax haven IBC to act as intermediary. The trader sells its products to the tax haven IBC on paper for, say, €800,000. The tax haven IBC would then sell the goods to the eventual customers for €1,000,000. The tax haven IBC would therefore show a profit of €200,000 but assuming it's a 0% tax haven there should be no tax charge.

The trading company would realize a profit of €200,000 as it sold the goods for €800,000 and incurred costs of €600,000.

The use of a re-invoicing strategy would save the trading company being taxed on €200,000, which could equate to a tax saving of €60,000.

Where is the Re-invoicing Company Incorporated?

The re-invoicing company is usually formed in one of the Caribbean tax haven jurisdictions (often combined with a nominee company incorporated in a less high-profile environment). So you'd be looking at the British Virgin Islands, the Bahamas, St Kitts Nevis etc, given that they provide a sound tax environment for import/export companies.

The main problem with this type of scheme is transfer pricing. The disposal by a trading company to the re-invoicing company is traditionally at a discount to allow a profit to be made overseas. In countries with strong transfer pricing requirements, this would need to be justified (for example because of additional services still to be provided by the re-invoicing company). Given that transfer pricing is a specialist area, it is essential that specific advice from a suitable specialist is obtained.

This is not the only problem with this re-invoicing strategy – remember the anti-avoidance rules that we looked at earlier? Well in this case the tax haven IBC could easily be classed as a controlled foreign company if it falls foul of the CFC conditions (for example, for US tax purposes if its shares are owned by US residents).

This would result in the profits of the tax haven IBC being subject to tax along with the international trading company. For this reason, re-invoicing is a difficult strategy to get passed the tax authorities, although you'll need to take detailed advice on the implications for your particular country of residence.

CHAPTER 9

HOW TO AVOID THE EU SAVINGS TAX DIRECTIVE

This had the potential to be a huge blow to EU residents having offshore bank accounts. As part of the EU's attempt to crack down on tax evasion, the EU Savings Tax Directive (ESD) was implemented as from 1 July 2005.

The ESD is an agreement between the member States of the EU to automatically exchange information with each other about customers who earn savings income in one EU member sate but actually reside in another.

Put simply, this means that if you live in the EU and have a bank account in any other EU country, details of you and the interest you earn will be passed to the tax authorities in your home country, who will undoubtedly check that you've been entering the information on your tax return. If you've not been declaring it, as a minimum they'll be likely to look for payment of the outstanding tax and interest, along with penalties.

Three of the EU states kicked up a fuss about this and have chosen to pull out. Austria, Belgium and Luxembourg have opted to apply alternative arrangements for the time being. They were then followed by many of the UK's Caribbean Crown Dependencies that are also caught by the directive.

Under these alternative arrangements, tax will be deducted at source from income earned by EU resident individuals on savings held in other countries covered by the directive.

Therefore under this option banks will automatically deduct tax from interest and other savings income earned and pass it to their local tax authority, indicating how much of the total amount relates to customers in each member state.

The rate of withholding tax is 15% from 1st July 2005, 20% from 1st July 2008 rising to 35% from 1st July 2011.

It's important to remember that states that go for the withholding tax option do so as an alternative to exchanging information. As such, the member state receiving the payments receives a bulk payment but does not receive personal details in respect of each individual. This will preserve confidentiality of customers overseas accounts.

As well as Austria, Belgium and Luxembourg opting for a withholding tax, other countries that have also now gone down this route (to preserve banking secrecy) include:

- Switzerland
- The Turks and Caicos Islands
- Liechtenstein
- The Channel Islands
- Monaco
- San Marino
- The British Virgin Islands
- Andorra

Even if you have an account in an overseas jurisdiction that applies the withholding option, you could if you wished 'contract out' of the withholding tax option and agree to the exchange of information with your country of residence.

It's also worth noting that exchange of information treaties and agreements with other countries following the G20 clampdown could in practice override banking secrecy in many of the countries that have opted for the withholding tax option.

Note that non-UK domiciliaries can be effectively exempt from the directive if they are taxed under the remittance basis. In this case they would usually need to apply to Revenue & Customs for a certificate to give to the overseas bank to ensure there is no withholding tax deducted (or exchange of information). However, following proposals introduced in the 2008 Finance Act to obtain this treatment from 6 April 2008 they would need to pay an annual £30,000 tax charge to Revenue & Customs (once they've been UK resident for at least seven of the past ten years).

The UK Government is also consulting on a new £50,000 tax charge for any non-UK domiciliaries who have been resident for at least 12 years.

Which Countries Are Affected

The ESD will apply to all EU member states. Great, you're thinking, I'll keep my cash in a Caribbean tax haven and avoid any withholding taxes.

Unfortunately, although the legal scope of the directive cannot extend outside the EU, it also affects:

- UK Crown Dependencies
- UK Overseas Territories
- Dependent Territories of The Netherlands
- Other 'Third Countries' that have volunteered to opt in

While most EU members have gone for the exchange of information option, most of the others have opted for the withholding tax (on the basis it will do least damage to the offshore industry).

The table below shows the countries and options chosen:

Withholding tax option	Exchange of info option
Channel Islands	UK
Belgium	Ireland
Luxembourg	Isle of Man
Austria	France
British Virgin Islands	Germany
Turks and Caicos Islands	Italy
Switzerland	Spain
Andorra	Portugal
Monaco	Greece
Liechtenstein	Sweden
San Marino	Finland
	Denmark
	Cyprus
	Czech Republic
	Estonia
	Hungary
	Latvia
	Lithuania
	Malta
	Poland
	Slovakia and Slovenia
	Anguilla
	Cayman Islands
	Montserrat

You'll see from the above that some of the EU's own low tax jurisdictions, notably Cyprus, the Isle of Man, Gibraltar and Malta will be exchanging information on interest receipts from EU residents.

In addition, the Caribbean tax havens of the Cayman Islands, Anguilla and Montserrat will also be exchanging information. This should come as no big hiccup if your overseas interest income is already being correctly declared in your tax return. Also some of the key tax havens such as Bermuda, Panama, Singapore, Barbados and the Bahamas are not included in the provisions.

Will the EU Savings Directive Be Extended?

It's been reported that EU tax officials aren't happy with the tax take from the scheme particularly from traditional tax havens in the Caribbean and are concerned that EU investors have simply transferred cash to countries that are outside the scope of the directive (particularly Singapore and Hong Kong).

As such the EU Commission is reported to have said that it wants to extend the Savings Directive to Hong Kong, Singapore, Japan, Macao, Bahrain, Dubai, Canada and the Bahamas.

Whether they will be successful will depend on the negotiations between the relevant countries. However it's well known that Singapore and Hong Kong are against adopting the directive. No doubt they'll mention the fact that they have already been very cooperative with the European states in terms of signing mutual legal assistance treaties and tax information agreements. In addition, the EU has released proposed amendments to the ESD. These are currently being consulted on, but it's anyone's guess when they will actually be implemented.

Will the ESD Affect You?

If you are an individual resident in an EU member state and earn bank interest or other savings income on investments held in one of the countries identified above, it is likely that you will be affected by the directive and will either be subject to the withholding tax or the exchange of information.

How Can the Terms of the Directive Be Avoided?

There are a number of ways that under the current provisions the obligations imposed by the directive could be avoided. In other words, where there would be no requirement to deduct a withholding tax or exchange information with your home state:

• Invest your cash in a bank account in a country not listed above and one in which another automatic exchange of information agreement is not in place.

• This could include: Labuan, Panama, Hong Kong, America, the Bahamas, Bermuda, Antigua and St Kitts and Nevis. Since the ESD has been implemented there has been a flood of cash going to Singapore and Hong Kong, both of which are not covered by the directive. As stated above, the EU Commission has considered talking with the authorities in some of these countries although the initial view is that they're not keen to implement the directive.

• Become a non-EU resident and you can invest your cash anywhere you want. The ESD will then not apply to any income earned from your investments.

• The ESD only applies to 'individuals'. One option if you are an EU resident would be to use a company (either onshore or offshore) to make the investments. The company would then not be subject to the terms of the ESD and the rules of your domestic regime would apply. If an offshore IBC was used, perhaps in conjunction with an offshore trust or foundation, you would need to review your domestic tax regime to ascertain whether you had any filing responsibilities.

• The ESD only applies to 'interest payments'. This is drafted widely to include 'debt claims of every kind'. This will therefore include income from:

• Government securities
• Bonds or debentures
• Accrued and capitalized interest

The big omission here is that it won't apply to dividends from shares or capital gains. Therefore careful choosing of investments could literally reap dividends! Investing in overseas equities as opposed to cash would avoid the terms of the ESD and you could also consider an investment bond with an offshore insurance company which would also be outside the scope of the ESD.

In some EU countries, including the UK, this can also offer other tax benefits including a reduction in income tax. Most hedge fund investments will also be outside the ESD.

Future Extension of Directive

As stated above the EU Commission is not happy with the number of loopholes in the current directive and they have proposed a number of amendments to 'tighten' up the rules.

Some of the changes include proposals to:

• Increase the amount of data exchanged between EU members on accounts held outside an EU resident's home country.
• Extend the definition of interest to various collective investments such as non-UCITS, hedge funds, private equity, structured products, insurance bonds and fixed annuities.
• Restrict the use of intermediaries to avoid tax by handling interest payments on behalf of EU residents.
• Tie in information exchange mechanisms to anti-money-laundering regulations to more easily identify the beneficial owners of accounts.

We'll need to wait for details of the specific provisions to be implemented to see what opportunities remain to invest overseas outside the terms of the directive.

CHAPTER 10

THE TREMENDOUS BENEFITS OF DOUBLE TAX TREATIES

Double tax treaties offer some substantial benefits to individuals and businesses that have international income.

A double tax treaty (DTT) is essentially an agreement between two countries that determines which country has the right to tax you in specified situations. The purpose behind this is to avoid double taxation.

It would be easy for a resident of one country to have income that arises in a second country. In this case both countries may want to tax the income (country 1 on the residence basis and country 2 on the source basis). This is where a DTT may come into play.

A treaty may state, for example, that certain types of capital gains should only be taxed in the country of residence, as opposed to the country where the asset is located. Or it may specifically provide for tax paid in one country to be deducted from the tax bill in another country.

However, the potential benefits of double tax treaties go far beyond this simple example.

What the Typical DTT Provisions Really Mean

I don't know if you've ever looked at a double tax treaty but they can be extremely difficult to follow. Most of the UK DTTs follow the standard OECD formula and below I've highlighted some of the most common provisions.

Some of the provisions are self explanatory but are worth stating in case you ever want to review a tax treaty on your own.

The first couple of articles usually look at what taxes the treaty will apply to and define any terms that are to be used.

Article I - Taxes Covered

It's always worthwhile checking that the tax you're interested in is expressly stated in this section. It will say here exactly which taxes in both states the treaty applies to. So, for example, the UK-Cyprus treaty states that it covers income tax and corporation tax in the UK and just income tax in Cyprus (no mention of capital gains tax). On the other hand, the UK-France treaty covers UK income tax, capital gains tax and corporation tax, along with French income and corporation tax.

Note that you won't find inheritance tax covered in these treaties. Inheritance tax treaties are completely separate and not as common as the income and corporation tax treaties. Treaties that cover inheritance tax are usually known as 'estate and gift tax' treaties. These focus on determining in which country an individual is subject to inheritance tax/estate tax and also on the location of assets for the purposes of charging estate taxes as well as providing for various exemptions.

In terms of the income tax treaties, it's from Article IV onwards, though, that you'll find the really important stuff.

Article IV – Residence

This article will determine where you are resident for tax purposes if you are a resident of two or more countries under the domestic tax laws of the countries concerned (this is commonly referred to as the 'treaty tie-breaker rules').

The OECD model treaty provides that:

- If you have a permanent home in one state, you are resident in that state.
- If you have a permanent home in both states, you are resident in the state which is your 'centre of vital interests' – the country in which you have close personal and financial ties.
- If you do not have a permanent home in either state and it is not possible to determine your centre of vital interests, you are resident in the country where you have an 'habitual abode'.

So, if you are a resident of two countries based on their domestic rules, you would look at these tests to find out which country you are 'treaty resident' in to determine which country has the right to tax you.

Becoming Treaty Resident Abroad

An individual who is 'treaty resident' overseas is simply treated as non-resident for the purposes of the treaty.

So, in the case of a UK resident individual treated as treaty resident overseas (eg by having their permanent home overseas) this means they are entitled to make claims for relief from UK tax as provided for under the agreement on the basis that they are a resident of the other State. As a result:

• Income or a gain of a type which is dealt with in the agreement and which arises in the overseas country is always exempt from UK tax.

• Income arising in other overseas territories is exempt if the agreement has an 'other income' Article.

• Only UK source income can be taxed and then only to the extent that such income can be taxed in the hands of a sole resident of the other country. Special rules however apply where any income (including foreign income) is connected with a business or profession which is carried on in the UK.

How the Tie Breaker Rules Apply

Permanent Home

An individual will be considered resident in the country where they have their permanent home. For individuals with only one permanent home, this is easy to establish.

The OECD commentary defines a permanent home as a permanent place of abode. So it could be simply a furnished room but it would need to be available continuously.

The OECD commentary states:

"As regards the concept of home, it should be observed that any form of home may be taken into account (house or apartment belonging to or rented by the individual, rented furnished room).

But the permanence of the home is essential; this means that the individual has arranged to have the dwelling available to him at all times continuously, and not occasionally for the purpose of a stay which, owing to the reasons for it, is necessarily of short duration (travel for pleasure, business travel, educational travel, attending a course at a school, etc.)."

Therefore to start with one looks for the country where there is a permanent home. If the individual has a permanent home in more than one country (or in no country) then you would look at the next test.

Centre of Vital Interests

The centre of vital interests test involves looking at an individual's personal and economic ties to determine to which country they are closer.
The OECD commentary states that you need to look at all of the factors surrounding an individual's lifestyle:

"The circumstances must be examined as a whole, but it would be nevertheless obvious that considerations based on the personal aspects of the individual must receive special attention. If a person who has a home in one State sets up a second in the other State while retaining the first, the fact that he retains the first in the environment where he has always lived, where he has worked, and where he has his family and possessions, can, together with other elements, go to demonstrate that he has retained his center of vital interests in the first State."

Therefore an individual's centre of vital interest does not shift easily from one country to another.

Habitual Abode

If residency can't be resolved based on either of the above tests, then residency is determined based on the individual's habitual abode. An individual's 'habitual abode' is the state where the individual spent the most time.

According to OECD commentary, the comparison must cover a sufficient length of time for it to be possible to determine whether the residence in either of the two states is habitual and to establish the intervals at which the stays took place.

Nationality

If a habitual abode exists in both states (or in neither) you'll assess treaty residence based on the country of citizenship. If an individual is a citizen of both states (or neither) treaty residence would usually be settled by the tax authorities of the relevant countries.

Note though that not all agreements will follow these tie breaker rules. The agreement with the Gambia for instance provides:

"...For the purposes of this Convention, the term 'resident of a territory' means subject to the provisions of paragraph (2) of this Article, any person who, under the law of that territory, is liable to taxation therein by reason of his domicile, residence, place of management or any other criterion of a similar nature. The terms 'resident of the United Kingdom' and 'resident of The Gambia' shall be construed accordingly..."

This is therefore stating that an individual is a resident of one country if he is liable to tax due to his domicile, residence, place of management or any other criterion of a similar nature.

This means there are no tie breaker rules as above and reinforces how important it is to actually check the terms of any particular treaty.

Article V – Permanent Establishment

This looks at the definition of a permanent establishment. This is crucial for international traders as it will frequently dictate the extent to which overseas trading activities will be taxed in an overseas jurisdiction. We'll look at this in a bit more detail shortly.

Article VI – Income from Real Property

Typically real property is land and property, so this article would cover the treatment of rental income. In practically all treaties the source country (where the property is located) is given the right to tax rental income from the property, along with the country of residence. As no exemption is provided in the treaty, relief from double tax will usually be given by way of a tax credit for any overseas tax paid.

Article XI – Interest

This article looks at the position where interest is paid by a resident of one country to a resident of another. The treaty between the two countries would usually look to either reduce any withholding taxes paid in the country where the interest is paid from, or state that the interest is exempt in the country of source.

Article XIII – Capital Gains

This is the article that is of most importance for property investors looking to emigrate and sell up. It covers capital gains from the disposal of assets. In many cases there is a catch-all provision that capital gains remain taxable ONLY in the seller's country of residence, except for land which can also typically be taxed in the country where the land is located and some shareholdings.

Article XIV – Independent Personal Services

This article looks at the taxation of income earned by self-employed people. If an individual has a 'fixed base' in another country, that country may tax any income that arises directly from that fixed base in a similar way that a business is taxed on profits from overseas permanent establishments.

Article XV – Dependent Personal Services

This looks at the taxation of employment income. In many treaties if the income is paid by a foreign employer and the employee is not physically present in the UK for more than 183 days, the income will only be taxable in the employee's country of residence.

Article XXIV – Elimination of Double Taxation

This allows what is already incorporated into UK tax law: the foreign tax credit.

This article is a catch-all that prevents double taxation with respect to income not addressed above and allows a deduction for overseas tax paid.

Article XXVII – Exchange of Information

This article is an agreement between the tax authorities to swap information to prevent tax evasion.

All in all, the terms of double tax treaties can be immensely complex, although on a simple level they can provide for one country to have primary taxing rights over certain sources of income and gains. This is often more attractive than being subject to tax in both countries and then claiming a tax credit for the overseas tax paid.

Permanent Establishment

Usually if an individual has business activities in Country X which does not have a tax treaty with his country of residence, Country Y, the domestic tax laws of Country X will apply when deciding where the profits of the business will be taxed. This will usually mean the profits will be fully taxed in Country X.

However, if there is a double tax treaty between Country X (country of residence) and Country Y (country where business activities carried out) business profits are not taxed in Country Y if there is no permanent establishment in Country Y – the profits will only be taxed in Country X where the trader is resident.

By contrast if a permanent establishment does exist in the overseas country, only the income derived from that permanent establishment is taxable.

This is clearly of great benefit to international traders as it could restrict their tax liability in overseas jurisdictions.

What is a Permanent Establishment?

The definition of a permanent establishment varies from treaty to treaty. Generally, the determination of whether a permanent establishment exists depends on two key issues:

- The existence of a fixed place of business

- The presence of dependent agents

If a business has a facility such as a branch, an office, a factory, a construction site and so on, it will usually be deemed to have a permanent establishment. However, even if the business has one of these, it will not be deemed to have a permanent establishment if the facility is used solely for 'preparatory or auxiliary' activities.

If a business has an agent in a treaty country who operates on its behalf and who exercises authority on its behalf to conclude contracts, this would indicate that there is a permanent establishment.

Not all types of agents would be caught within the permanent establishment rules. A notable exception is commission agents who might generate orders but don't have the authority to actually bind the 'principal'.

How to Avoid Overseas Activities Being Classed as a Permanent Establishment

- Only carry out 'preparatory or auxiliary' activities. As mentioned above, a business won't have a permanent establishment if its activities in the treaty country amount to just 'preparatory or auxiliary' activities.

- In order to get classed within this category you'd be looking at activities that lead up to future trading – for example, making enquiries or 'testing the water' in overseas markets.

- Shortening the duration of construction, installation or consultancy projects. Whether a construction, installation or consultancy project constitutes a permanent establishment usually depends on how long the project lasts. For example, some treaties provide that a permanent establishment includes activities that continue for a period of more than six months. Provided you can ensure your activity in a particular country is less than this, there may be no permanent establishment.

- Using independent agents to carry out business. Tax treaties usually provide that using agents will not constitute a permanent establishment. Typical provisions provide that:

"an enterprise of a Contracting State shall not be deemed to have a permanent establishment in the other Contracting State merely because it carries on business in that other State through a broker, general commission agent or any other agent of an independent status, provided that such a person is acting in the ordinary course of his business."

In view of this, it's worth considering the advantages of using independent agents to carry out business in other countries. (Note that in addition to the potential tax benefits, there are other benefits in using independent agents to carry out business, for example better knowledge of local customers.)

Dividends, Interest and Royalties

As we've already seen, many overseas countries will not only try to tax your business profits but will also levy a withholding tax on dividends paid to shareholders.

As a result, the total foreign taxes payable in an overseas country may be much higher than the income or corporation tax you suffer in your home jurisdiction.

This is where tax treaties come to the rescue. They can help to alleviate this problem by providing reduced rates of withholding tax on dividends.

Usually tax treaties provide relief in the form of lower tax rates for interest income or royalties and this may give rise to tax planning opportunities.

Example

Investco, resident in Country 3, is thinking of investing in Country 1. Investco also has a subsidiary (Subsidco) in Country 2. If the withholding tax rate between Country 1 and 2 is lower than that between Country 1 and the 3, Investco may consider using its subsidiary in Country 2 to carry out the investment, to take advantage of the lower withholding tax rate.

At this point it's worth mentioning 'treaty shopping'. If the arrangement in the above example has no commercial purpose other than avoiding taxes, it might be regarded as 'treaty shopping'.

Treaty shopping involves the use of a tax treaty by a person who is a resident of a third country (in other words not a resident of one of the two countries covered by the tax treaty).

A common example of this is the use of the Netherlands to route royalty income to benefit from the lower rates of withholding tax.

The problem of treaty shopping is worst for countries like the US which has withholding taxes which vary from treaty to treaty. As a result taxpayers have frequently taken advantage of the most favourable treaty.

However, all recent tax treaties entered into by the US include what's known as a limitation on benefits article. The main purpose of this article is to deny treaty benefits to a company that is resident in one of the treaty countries but is in effect serving as a channel for residents of a third country.

If the article applies it will prevent the lower withholding taxes applying. So this could easily scupper any plans for using treaties to obtain lower withholding taxes. Note this problem only arises if there is a limitation of benefits article.

Elimination of double taxation

One of the basic objectives of tax treaties is to prevent income being taxed twice. This objective is generally achieved by an 'elimination of double taxation' provision which usually has similar wording to the following clause from the double tax treaty between the UK and Spain:

"Where a resident of Spain derives income which, in accordance with the provisions of this Convention, may be taxed in the United Kingdom, Spain shall allow as a deduction from the tax on the income of that person an amount equal to the tax paid in the United Kingdom – such deduction shall not, however, exceed that part of the tax, as computed before the deduction is given, which is appropriate to the income derived from the United Kingdom. The tax paid in the United Kingdom shall also be allowed as a deduction against the corresponding Spanish prepayment taxes."

In essence this ensures you aren't taxed twice on the same income. In the case of the UK this provision is actually pretty superfluous as the UK operates its own system of double tax relief. This means that even if there is no double tax treaty in existence, a UK resident with overseas income would still usually get double tax relief.

The elimination of withholding taxes makes an effective treaty network a valuable weapon in any tax minimisation 'arsenal'.

This is particularly the case for offshore groups and for international trading, particularly in a group structure. This is where many tax havens fail to deliver as they are unlikely to have any established treaty network. Instead countries such as the UK, Cyprus, Ireland and Gibraltar offer great opportunities.

Overseas Workers

If you're going overseas on a secondment you should also look at the relevant double tax treaty to see if it can yield any tax benefits.

In the case of the UK, overseas workers who come to the UK and spend between six and twelve months in the UK may be able to make use of a suitable double tax treaty with the country they come from.

Certain treaties will allow salary to be exempted from UK tax if a worker's presence in the UK is less than 183 days during the tax year.

However, in order to qualify for this exemption the worker will need to satisfy a couple of conditions:

- Firstly, they must be tax resident in the other country.
- Secondly, the employer must be a non-UK employer who doesn't recharge the UK company for the worker's services and shouldn't claim a UK tax deduction for the UK salary.

Each treaty is different so you'll need to examine the particular treaty between your home country and where you'll be working to see if you qualify. Some treaties prevent tax year straddling by specifying that the presence in the UK must be for less than 183 days.

Avoiding Capital Gains Tax (CGT)

UK residents usually pay CGT on their worldwide capital gains.
Tax planners used to suggest becoming non-resident/not ordinarily resident for one tax year and disposing of assets before returning to the UK.

The UK Government subsequently tightened up the rules and now it is pretty much impossible to escape capital gains tax by leaving the country for a short time.

A UK resident would now normally need to be non UK resident for more than five complete tax years to avoid paying capital gains tax on profits.

In the period to April 5th following your departure, your gains are taxed in the year the gain arises. From April 6th after your departure to the date of your return, your gains are usually taxed in the year you return (unless your are not resident for more than five full tax years or the gain is from assets bought and sold while not resident).

Therefore if you're UK resident, you'll be subject to the five year non residence requirement to avoid UK capital gains tax, irrespective of what any double tax treaty says.

CHAPTER 11

OTHER IMPORTANT TAX HAVEN BENEFITS

Deemed Uplift on Immigration

As we've seen tax havens essentially fall into three categories:

- Nil tax havens such as the Bahamas and British Virgin Islands
- Low tax havens such as Malta and Gibraltar
- Countries operating a territorial exemption such as Panama and Costa Rica

However, any discussion of tax havens wouldn't be complete without looking at the full picture and considering some of the other ways that other countries allow you to minimise your tax burden.

Certain high-tax countries also offer rules that could help you slash your tax bill – it's just a case of knowing how to use them. For example, some countries such as Australia can offer what's known as a deemed uplift in the value of your assets on immigration. This rule can save you thousands in capital gains tax.

Although you may have bought an asset for next to nothing years ago, your cost for tax purposes in your new country of residence is deemed to be the market value at the date of immigration.

In most cases this means that if you sell the asset shortly after obtaining residence you will not realise a gain – the selling price and the 'cost' will be roughly the same (the market value of the asset).

All that will be taxed is any gain that has arisen since the date of immigration.

This type of planning can usually apply to either assets held personally or also assets held within a trust or other entity.

What Happens When You Leave the Country?

The other side of this tax break is that if the immigrant subsequently leaves the country there is then likely to be a deemed disposal of assets at the date of emigration (known as an 'exit tax').

Note that in Australia a special election can be made to avoid this.

The EU has taken exception to exit taxes and has challenged them in the EU court. Austria, Denmark, France, Norway, Germany and The Netherlands have imposed a form of exit tax. The EU challenged the French exit tax and found it was against EU law. Based on this The Netherlands amended its exit tax regime.

Continuing Liabilities

Just because you cease to be a resident of a particular country does not mean that it will cease to take an interest in you.

In the UK, for example, an expatriate may be liable to capital gains tax on assets held at departure if sold within six UK tax years and you return within that period. Countries such as Spain and Germany will continue to tax certain expatriates for a number of years if they move to a tax haven jurisdiction.

Others such as Iceland will tax the expatriate for a while until they become resident in another jurisdiction – sometimes in these circumstances it may be useful and quite easy to obtain resident status in a favourable tax jurisdiction such as Gibraltar or Malta (by making use of the HNWI or permanent residence schemes). The Netherlands applies a 10-year deemed residence rule for the purposes of its estate taxes, which has recently been confirmed as in agreement with EU law by the EU Court.

The European Tax Havens

We've covered a lot of the Caribbean tax havens and whilst many of these offer 0% tax it's important to note that for individuals living in Europe there are lots of opportunities closer to home.

The EU Parent/Subsidiary Directive on dividends can be a useful tool. In particular, an increasing trend is for certain EU countries such as Malta and Cyprus to be used as a channel for interest and royalty income arising outside the EU. Crucially the directive doesn't contain a limitation on benefits clause which makes it much more beneficial for use as channel for funds.

As we've seen Cyprus is a particularly good choice for investments in Eastern Europe given its strong treaty network and many provide for 0% withholding tax on interest, royalties and dividends. This can therefore allow the disposal of property in Eastern Europe and the extraction of proceeds free of taxes.

Cyprus itself offers a highly advantageous capital gains regime with no gain charged on the disposal of shares or land unless the land is located in Cyprus or the shares are in a Cyprus property investment/dealing company.

Malta can also be considered a potential low tax jurisdiction and in terms of lifestyle it's popular due to the low property prices, low crime rate and Mediterranean climate.

Another less well known European tax haven is Estonia. An Estonian company pays no tax on its income and shares can often be sold free of taxes. Instead Estonian companies only pay corporation tax (at a rate of 21%) when profits are distributed to shareholders. If profits are retained in the company there is no company tax charge.

Ireland, the Isle of Man and the Channel Islands are also becoming of increasing importance. Ireland has a very good network of double tax treaties and a low rate of tax (with Irish residents having a very low tax burden). The Isle of Man and the Channel Islands offer a low rate of personal income tax but more importantly offer a 0% rate of corporation tax.

There are also other changes in various other EU states which are intended to increase revenues. In Spain for instance in 2013 and 2014 savings income is subject to a progressive tax rate from 21% to 27% (increased from a flat rate of 19% on the first €6,000 and 19% above this).

Germany has also announced some significant changes to its corporate tax system from 2009, including a reduction in the rate of corporation tax to 15%. There is also a flat rate tax of 25% for individual's investment income.

Investing in the UK

The UK has become a hot spot for property investment and many non-residents want to know how to invest in the UK whilst minimising their UK tax.

A non-resident should be able to structure his investment so that no income tax, capital gains tax or inheritance tax is payable. A common plan is to use a nil tax trust (for example, in the Channel Islands) to invest through a zero tax company (for example, in the British Virgin Islands) which would lend money to the company. The company would be allowed a deduction for the interest.

You need to be careful about this and only provide debt to the extent a third party would. The Revenue will generally accept a loan of 75-85% of the cost, charged on the property. The interest deduction would in practice significantly reduce or even eliminate the UK taxable profits, particularly if an interest only loan was used. As the property is owned by an offshore IBC there would be no question of UK capital gains tax or inheritance tax being levied.

Certificates of Tax Exemption

Some tax havens, particularly the Caribbean ones, offer what's known as 'certificates of tax exemption'. Essentially these are a promise by the government that no tax will be levied on your income or gains whilst you are a resident (usually for a certain number of years, such as 20 years).

These exemptions give you some certainty in your affairs which is valuable considering the expense of setting up an offshore structure.

Countries such as the Bahamas, British Virgin Islands, St Kitts and Nevis and Panama all offer exemptions.

New Zealand and Australian Tax Changes

Aside from the traditional tax haven jurisdictions, New Zealand and Australia have introduced provisions that can prove very tax-efficient for new residents.

New Zealand

New immigrants to New Zealand (NZ) qualify for an automatic tax exemption on their overseas income under the Taxation Act 2006.

This works by exempting all 'transitional residents' from NZ tax on their foreign-sourced income by treating it as if it were received by a non-NZ resident.

To be classed as a 'transitional resident' you need to ensure that you arrive in NZ after 1 April 2006 and that:

- You have a permanent residence in NZ, and

- Immediately before acquiring that residence you were non-resident for at least 10 years, and

- You haven't previously been classed as a transitional resident.

If you can satisfy these conditions (which shouldn't be too difficult) you'll be classed as a transitional resident for four years, and you'll be classed as a 'normal' resident on the 48th month after the month in which you acquired permanent residence.

What's the benefit of this transitional residence status?

It means that your foreign sourced income is exempt from New Zealand tax. In general the only types of foreign income not tax exempt will be overseas employment income and certain types of business income.

Therefore if you derive much of your income from investments you'll see some massive benefits. In particular, interest income, dividends as well as employment and bonus income from a previous employment are exempt.

After the four-year period has ended foreign source income is then taxed in New Zealand at rates of up to 39%.

During the first four years though, you should be subject to much lower taxes in New Zealand due to the exemption for overseas income.

If you're planning to move from the UK to New Zealand, provided you establish yourself as non-UK resident you would be exempt from UK taxes on any overseas sourced income. As such, if you received interest from an offshore account it should be free of UK and New Zealand income tax. Similarly, any dividends received from overseas companies should be free of both UK and New Zealand taxes.

In fact even if you received UK interest or dividends from UK companies you should still be able to secure a zero tax position as there is an effective exemption for non-UK residents from UK income tax in these circumstances.

So obtaining New Zealand residence can be very beneficial in tax terms for company owners as well as financial investors.

Australia

Australia has introduced a 'temporary resident' status. Unlike permanent residents, temporary residents are not taxed on overseas source income or gains as from July 2006. Similar to the New Zealand transitional resident provisions, this can be a very advantageous tax status to obtain.

A temporary resident is defined as someone who holds a temporary visa and who is also not an Australian citizen (and whose spouse is not an Australian citizen).

The Concept of Domicile

Aside from residence, sometimes a country will use the concept of domicile which will have an impact on how residents are subject to tax.

Domicile is a different concept from residence and in many countries it may not even be relevant. In the UK it is relevant for inheritance tax purposes as well for assessing the chargeability of overseas income and gains. It also has implications for estate tax in the USA.

Domicile implies a much stronger relationship with a country than simple residence. The residence test is usually satisfied by spending a certain number of days each tax year in a country. Domicile usually means that you make a country your permanent home. This is satisfied if you were born in the country or if you live there with the intention of making it your permanent home.

In jurisdictions such as the UK, Ireland and Barbados and Malta, an individual's liability to income tax will be affected by their domicile status. In these countries there is a clear distinction between a person's domicile and physical residence for tax purposes. In effect, a 'foreign' person resident in, for example, the UK or Ireland will only be taxed on foreign income sent back to the UK or Ireland.

These countries therefore offer excellent opportunities for immigrants to minimise taxes where they have income that is generated offshore. In the UK though, the benefit of these rules has been restricted for any non domiciliaries that are long term residents of the UK.

Once a foreigner has been in the UK for seven years they can only avoid UK tax by keeping income abroad if they pay a £30,000 tax charge to the UK tax authorities. Since 6th April 2012 this has been increased to £50,000 for non domiciliaries who have been UK resident for at least twelve years.

Some countries such as Japan apply a similar concept to domicile. Japan, for example, generally only taxes non-permanent residents on their Japanese source income and on foreign income that is remitted to Japan.

Individuals will be non permanent residents provided they do not intend to permanently reside in Japan and have resided in Japan for fewer than five years.

Capital and Income Accounts

A common technique to maximise the use of non domicile status is to use separate income and capital accounts.

This allows a distinction to be made between capital and subsequent income from capital (such as interest) before taking up permanent residence and can even allow tax free living in the above countries in certain cases.

It is often advisable for foreign domiciliaries to have at least three overseas bank accounts:

- The first account for existing capital
- The second account to deposit the proceeds of any asset disposals
- The third account to contain the interest from the first two accounts, along with any other foreign source income

The point of this exercise is to segregate your foreign income and gains.

If you want to bring money into the country you should first remit funds from the first account. This can usually be done free of tax.

If further funds are required, then withdrawals can be made from the second account, which could effectively subject the withdrawals to capital gains tax. However, this would depend on your country of residence. Malta for example would not tax these gains and in the UK and Ireland there would be reliefs to reduce any tax payable.

Finally, withdrawals from the third account would be subject to income tax.

Tax Sparing Provisions

We touched on these earlier in the book – they allow a deduction for taxes that have not actually been suffered.

This applies so that if tax is 'spared' or exempted in one country, then it is credited against your tax bill in your home country as if it had actually been paid in the first country.

The purpose of these provisions is usually to encourage foreign investment in developing countries. These provisions encourage direct foreign investments in the tax sparing country as the foreign investors enjoy a better return on their money because of the potential tax credit they can get from their home authorities.

Example – Malaysia

Malaysian tax treaties often include 'tax sparing' arrangements. A dividend that is distributed out of profits which have been exempted from tax under the Malaysian tax incentive regime, is deemed to be paid out of profits that have been subject to tax. This is so as to enable a non-resident to claim a tax credit on the exempt dividend in his home country. This also applies to interest on certain loans and royalties.

Cyprus

Cyprus has some extremely favourable tax sparing provisions which apply to the following countries:

- Canada
- Czech Republic
- Denmark
- Egypt
- Germany
- Greece
- India
- Ireland

- Italy
- Malta
- Poland
- Romania
- United Kingdom

However, these provisions look like they are now on their way out. The OECD has recommended that they be abolished given the potential for abuse although they're currently still going strong.

Offshore Bank Accounts

In my experience, the four reasons why people set up offshore accounts are:

- Tax avoidance
- Higher interest rates
- Asset protection
- Privacy requirements

Let's have a look at each one in a little more detail.

Tax Avoidance

A common fallacy is that you can just bank your cash offshore and avoid tax on any income generated. This is not the case for residents of practically all developed countries unless you're lucky enough to be in a state that taxes on the basis of territoriality (for example, Panama, Costa Rica, or Singapore).

As tracking offshore accounts can prove difficult for tax authorities, the EU Savings Tax Directive now makes it easier for governments to get their share of taxes due. As we've seen, under this regime tax is automatically deducted from interest payable in many European (and some Caribbean) countries. This doesn't stop individuals still having a duty to declare the overseas interest (although there would usually be credit for any overseas tax deducted).

If you want to avoid overseas tax being automatically deducted from interest you have to ensure that your offshore account is in a country not subject to the directive. This could include:

- The Bahamas (check out Bahamian accounts with First Caribbean International Bank).

- Panama (Banco General HSBC Panama, Banco National). The standard interest rates are around 1%.

- Hong Kong (HSBC and Bank of China with rates of less than 1%).

- Singapore (DBS or Maybank with rates of up to 1%).

There is a significant difference between these rates and the Channel Islands and Isle of Man offshore bank rates, which tend to be much higher. It will therefore only be if avoiding the European Savings Tax Directive and achieving privacy benefits are crucial factors that a personal account in one of these countries is going to be beneficial (this is only likely to apply to non-UK residents or non-UK domiciliaries).

Higher Interest Rates

Offshore saving accounts often offer attractive rates of interest. If you shop around you'll find rates in excess of 2.5%. If you're looking at fixed rate bonds, higher rates can be obtained. These tend to be available from banks in the Channel Islands, and as such would be subject to the European Savings Tax Directive.

Note that these are gross interest rates, unlike interest paid by UK banks or building societies, which usually has basic-rate tax deducted at source.

Of course if you are non-UK resident (as above) this would not be an issue, as you wouldn't be subject to income tax in the UK anyway. You would then need to consider whether there would be any overseas tax in your country of residence.

Asset Protection

Having an offshore bank account on its own probably wouldn't offer much in the way of asset protection, as any court would class cash held in an offshore account as yours.

If you are serious about ring-fencing assets you must set up an offshore structure, including an offshore company, offshore bank account and probably an offshore trust as well. Even this won't guarantee that your assets will be protected, but it will at least give you a fighting chance, provided you set it up properly. For example, where possible the trust holding the overseas company should not have you as a beneficiary. Any distributions should be to family members with no 'history' of distributions to you.

Establishing the trust as a bona fide arrangement is essential to showing the whole structure is not a sham arrangement, with the trust assets being classed as yours.

If you're going for an offshore structure Panama is probably one of the best options. A Panama trust or foundation, holding a company with a Panamanian bank account is a sound choice.

Privacy Requirements

Privacy is totally different from asset protection. When considering privacy you're essentially looking at how difficult it is for someone else (for example, a disgruntled business associate or ex-spouse) to gain information about your bank accounts.

The Swiss numbered account was always seen as the epitome of banking privacy and if you're interested they're still available from various Swiss banks. Having said that, numbered accounts are not anonymous accounts and the bank will still need to verify your identity and the source of funds (to satisfy money-laundering rules). In addition, these accounts will still be subject to a withholding tax under the ESD (which has increased to 35% from July 2011).

In addition the G20 and OECD clampdown on the exchange of information between different countries will now make it more difficult to genuinely offer a 100% private offshore bank account. Practically all countries will agree to exchange information on the signatories and holders of offshore bank accounts, which reinforces the fact that you should ensure you fully comply with the disclosure requirements in your home country.

ABOUT THE AUTHOR

Lee Hadnum LLB ACA CTA is an international tax specialist. He is a Chartered Accountant and Chartered Tax Adviser and is the Editor of the popular tax planning website:

www.wealthprotectionreport.co.uk

Lee is also the author of a number of best selling tax planning books.

OTHER TAX GUIDES

- **Tax Planning Techniques Of The Rich & Famous** - Essential reading for anyone who wants to use the same tax planning techniques as the most successful Entrepreneurs, large corporations and celebrities

- **The Worlds Best Tax Havens 2014/2015**– 230 page book looking at the worlds best offshore jurisdictions in detail

- **Non Resident & Offshore Tax Planning 2014/2015**– Offshore tax planning for UK residents or anyone looking to purchase UK property or trade in the UK. A comprehensive guide.

- **Tax Planning With Offshore Companies & Trusts 2014/2015: The A-Z Guide** - Detailed analysis of when and how you can use offshore companies and trusts to reduce your UK taxes

- **Tax Planning For Company Owners 2014/2015**– How company owners can reduce income tax, corporation tax and NICs

- **How To Avoid CGT In 2014/2015** – Tax planning for anyone looking to reduce UK capital gains tax

- **Buy To Let Tax Planning 2014/2015** – How property investors can reduce income tax, CGT and inheritance tax

- **Asset Protection Handbook** – Looks at strategies to ringfence your assets in today's increasing litigious climate

- **Working Overseas Guide** – Comprehensive analysis of how you can save tax when working overseas

- **Double Tax Treaty Planning** – How you can use double tax treaties to reduce UK taxes

Made in the USA
Lexington, KY
08 October 2015